The Air War
Over Lowestoft
1939 – 1945

A diary of the principal wartime
aviation events

The Air War Over Lowestoft
1939-1945

A diary of the principal wartime aviation events

Bob Collis
Simon Baker

Foreword by Richard Morling

Printed by Waveney Print

Published by Lowestoft Aviation Society

First published 1994
Reprinted August 2011
© Bob Collis
This edition published by Lowestoft Aviation Society 2011
All rights reserved
© Lowestoft Aviation Society 2011

Cover design: Andrew Farman (1967 - 2010)

Acknowledgments:

We would like to thank the following people who have helped us to produce this book, John Holmes, John Harris, Phillip Thacker, Cecil 'Dick' Wickham, Richard Reeve, Cleeve Bury, Martin Bowman, Andrew Farman, Denis Gilbert, Val Grimble, Stephen Webbe, Jeff Carless, Julian P Foynes and Peter Killby, Richard Morling for his foreword and L.A.S. Chairman Roger Smith. We would also like to take this opportunity to thank Peter Jenkins for kindly allowing us to use some of the photos taken by his late father, Ford Jenkins.

Finally, a special thank you to our wives and families for their patience with us over the, what occasionally felt like endless, time it has taken to write this book.

Photo Credits/Reference

The photographs and images used in this book have come from a number of sources and the appropriate credit is given where possible. Although every attempt has been made to establish the copyright for every illustration used this has not always been possible.

The material for this book has been researched and obtained from a number of sources including official military (both British and German), Police and civil defence records. Another important source of information, particularly when compiling the Roll of Honour, has been the Suffolk Record Office in Lowestoft Library.

The internet has increasingly become an invaluable research tool and the following websites have proved valuable in researching and checking information: www.8thafhs.org, website of the 8th Air Force Historical Society, www.453rd.com, website of the 453rd Bomb Group, www.bbc.co.uk/peopleswar, www.raf.mod.uk, website of the Royal Air Force, www.aicrewrememberancesociety.com and www.cwgc.org, website of the Commonwealth War Graves Commission.

Foreword

I would compliment Bob and Simon for producing this interesting and inform-
ative book on a period of the 20th century that is becoming part of history that
affected the lives of everyone living in Lowestoft at the time.

Being very young at the time I can only rely on documentary evidence such as
this, as all my family who were affected by the raids on Lowestoft during WW2,
are no longer with us. I do know that my maternal grandmother, was bombed
out of her home in Raglan Street, and her house in Royal Avenue was also
bombed, although at that time she was living with us in Derbyshire.

On my father's side the family business was first bombed on the night of 9th
April 1941. Being an evening raid there was no loss of life, but most of the shop
was destroyed and the business was temporally transferred across the road to
Rogers cycle shop. Stock, and the part of the shop that was not completely
destroyed, became unusable after another raid on 12th May. In the mean time
the family home on Old Nelson Street, was bombed on 3rd May, together with
pianos that had been stored there. All this made it difficult to pursue a war
damage claim. Times were difficult for many families in Lowestoft, my father,
Hugh, like many others, had now been called up, but they continued with the
move to 106 London Road North. Things ran fairly smoothly for a time with the
rota for fire watching and the general uncertainty of what was happening to
loved ones on active service. Then on 13th January 1942, came the 'Waller's
raid', the shop was completely destroyed, killing my grandfather Ernest, the
founder of the business, three members of staff and three customers who were
in the shop at the time.

The time was now even more difficult for my family, having lost their father
and their brother was known to be in Singapore, which fell to the Japanese on
15th February and his future was unknown, (he was captured by the Japanese
on 8th March 1942 and died in July 1943). With all this uncertainty they
decided to carry on the business and move to 139 High Street on 26th January.
Apparently, people were advised not to go to Morlings, as they got bombed!
  Our family story during WW2 is not unique as I am sure that many other
Lowestoft families have their own stories to tell. This book will be a valuable
resource in times to come, as we must not forget this period in the history of
Lowestoft.
Richard Morling

Preface

The sole vision of Lowestoft Aviation Society since it was formed around fifteen years ago, is to raise aviation awareness in the town and its surrounding area of air events past, present and future. Bob and Simon have ably caught the past in this book, outlining what happened in Lowestoft and the surrounding area during the period 1939 to 1945. There have been books covering the history of Lowestoft during the war years before; however, the key difference with this offering is that it concentrates on one specific part of the town's war history, the air war. As well as detailing what actually happened on the ground and in the air over England's most easterly town, it also covers, with a wide brush, the ebb and flow of the great air campaigns and the technological struggle taking place behind it.

There has never been a military airfield in Lowestoft, yet the aviation heritage of the town is great. During World War II the town's population had borne witness to the early Luftwaffe bombing of the port, and indeed other parts of the country, to the point where thousands of aircraft passed overhead daily, including British and American bombers flying around the clock. Finally came the last futile 'tip and run' air attacks by Luftwaffe fighter bombers, as the war in Europe drew to a close.

It had not been easy for the people of the town, many lost loved ones or their lives, and many more their homes. It is important in my opinion, that the events that led to their suffering and loss are put on record so that with the passing of time their sacrifice is not forgotten. Bob and Simon's diligent work goes a long way to ensure that this story does not fade with the passing of time.

Roger Smith
Chairman, Lowestoft Aviation Society - Suffolk's Eyes on the Skies

Introduction

When war was declared it was obvious to most people that Lowestoft would find itself in the front line of aerial attacks, indeed when Germany overran Holland the Luftwaffe had less than a thirty minute flight before they reached the town. This coupled with the fact that initially the town's anti-aircraft (AA) defences were limited, with the more important ports having first claim to the few guns available at the time, made the town an ideal target for surprise 'hit and run' attacks. Defences were eventually bolstered and as the Royal Navy made increasing use of the harbour, making it a military establishment, the number of AA guns increased. Of course the threat of attack from the air was not a new concept for the residents of Lowestoft. In WW1 the town was on three occasions the recipient of bombs dropped from Zeppelins and German sea-planes. The town was also shelled by warships of the German High Seas fleet in 1916, making Lowestoft possibly the only place in Britain to experience all three types of enemy offensive in the Great War. During the 1930's films like H G Wells' 'The shape of things to come' painted a horrific picture of the results of mass air attack on cities. The reality, when it came, was not as bad as had been feared, but it was bad enough.

As the war progressed the number of airfields in the region grew dramatically, especially with the arrival of the Americans. Lowestoft became an important landmark for Allied aircrew heading out on, and returning home from missions, and the sight of these large formations over the town became a familiar one. Lowestoft, like many towns throughout the country, established a 'Spitfire Fund' to buy one of the famous fighters, and was also affiliated to 107 Squadron, RAF.

This book is not intended as a definitive history of the air war over the town, nor does it concentrate solely on bombing raids. Not every incident or air-raid which took place is listed, to do such justice to the subject would require a book many times this size. Instead what we have tried to do is highlight the principal events, as well as some lesser known ones, and where possible, as information becomes available, bring them more up to date.

Air Raid Precautions (ARP) posts were an essential part of Britain's Civil Defence (CD) activities during WW2 As can be seen from this wartime map there were a significant number of posts in Lowestoft.

1939

From the moment war was declared on the 3rd September it was obvious Lowestoft would find itself in the front line. However, enemy air activity in the remaining months of the year, during the period known as the 'phoney war' was minimal.

3rd September 1939: At 11.15am the Prime Minister, Neville Chamberlain, made his radio announcement that Britain had declared war on Germany. A mere thirty minutes later, at 11.45am, the first air raid 'Alert' sounded at Lowestoft. Later stated to have been a test, this was the first of more than 2,000 such alerts in the town during the Second World War.

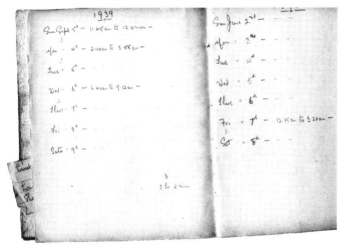

First of Many: the town's first Air Raid Alert on 3rd September 1939 recorded in a Royal Observer Corps log book. (Bob Collis)

17th October 1939: The first high flying enemy aircraft was spotted over Lowestoft during the afternoon, only 24 hours after the first Luftwaffe attacks against Great Britain in WW2. A reconnaissance aircraft, it was then plotted passing over Frostenden and Halesworth before heading out to sea between Aldeburgh and Orford. It returned and penetrated as far inland as Ipswich before finally crossing out between Felixstowe and Harwich. German reconnaissance aircraft intermittently over-flew the town by day and night throughout the war, demonstrating the enemy's interest in the area.

1940

The first few months of 1940 saw a continuation of 'the phoney war' however it did not last long with the first enemy bombs falling on the town in June. With the bombing came the inevitable casualties and fatalities and the harsh realisation that for many of the towns people things would never be the same. As the threat of invasion loomed and the danger from air raids increased, some 3,500 Lowestoft school children were evacuated, mainly to Derbyshire.

21st June 1940: Lowestoft found itself firmly at the front line of the air war when the first enemy bombs were dropped on the town at 1.30am. Two High Explosive (HE) bombs landed near Yarmouth Road, Gunton, and Gorleston Road. Although these bombs caused only slight damage and there were no casualties, they were the forerunners of a terrifying rain of death and destruction that was to batter the town over the next five years.

3rd July 1940: A Dornier Do 17 carried out the first daylight raid of the war on the town, which was possibly aimed at the Gasworks, at 4.30 pm. The first stick of seven 50kg HE bombs fell between the beach and Rant Score East. No air-raid warning preceded the raid, and three people were killed, one an 18 month old child, when the cottage they were in was hit and destroyed. The sirens were belatedly sounding when the same aircraft circled round and five minutes later dropped a further 12 bombs on the town centre. The Co-operative Wholesale Society (CWS) Central Store in Clapham Road was hit and a fire started which destroyed most of the building before the Auxiliary Fire Service (AFS) could bring it under control. This was the first of many of the town's landmark buildings to be destroyed.

Through the war 51 unexploded bombs (UXBs) were found in the town and the first of these, from this raid, was discovered lodged in an alleyway off Surrey Street. The Civil Defence and Air Raid Patrol (ARP) services evidently acquitted themselves well in this first baptism of fire, which sadly saw four people killed and 17 injured.

21st August 1940: At 4.12pm a Dornier Do 17Z dropped a long stick of bombs, which included a few incendiary bombs – the first on the town - between Gunton Drive and Stradbroke Road in Pakefield. While the material damage caused by the 12 50kg HE bombs was not great, sadly two air-raid shelters were hit; one at Harvey, Wilson and Osborne's Shipyard on Horn Hill, and the other at the rear of the Zephyr Engineering Works in Freemantle Road. As a result six people were killed and a further seven injured.

Enemy activity had been widespread with some 200 raids, carried out in most instances by single aircraft, plotted across the South and East coasts. The general summary of the Home Security Report for the 21st August stated *"There have been a large number of raids by small numbers of enemy aircraft, chiefly in the south and eastern districts. The objectives appear to have been aerodromes but indiscriminate bombing and machine gunning of open towns was apparent".*

6th September 1940: Whilst the Battle of Britain raged, predominantly over south east England, RAF Bomber Command was playing its part by taking the fight to the Germans. However, the limited range and capacity of the bombers available at the time meant that the results of these early raids were often poor. It was while returning from such a raid that a Hampden bomber from 44 Squadron, based at RAF Waddington, Lincolnshire, ditched in the sea quarter of a mile off Lowestoft at 5.43am, after running out of fuel having spent more than nine hours in the air on an exhausting night raid over Stettin (then part of Germany). The crew of four managed to escape uninjured and were brought ashore at Lowestoft by HM Trawler (HMT) *Ben Hur.* Not recorded at the time was the fact that the pilot, Pilot Officer David Romans DFC, had ditched another Hampden off the Norfolk coast, again through shortage of fuel, just five days earlier!

Down in the drink: this artist's impression by John Reeve of Mettingham shows Pilot Officer David Romans DFC and his crew about to ditch their Hampden bomber off Ness Point, Lowestoft in the early hours of 6th September 1940. Romans was killed on 8th September 1941 when his 90 Squadron B-17 Fortress I was shot down over Norway during one of the early high-altitude raids with this aircraft. (Reproduced courtesy John Reeve)

29th September 1940: On this date the east and south east of England were subjected to a series of attacks, with Lowestoft suffering the most damage. At 11.25am a Dornier Do 17Z flying at 20,000 feet dropped a stick of 18 x 50kg HE bombs, its target being the harbour. The majority of the bomb load fell harmlessly into the sea. However, the remaining six bombs fell across their target area, destroying and damaging a number of buildings. One bomb scored a direct hit on an office building at the Herring Market, Waveney Dock, killing four sailors and four civilians employed by the Royal Navy. The last bomb to fall landed on the pavement outside Marconi House on the corner of Battery Green Road and Grove Road, a hail of bomb splinters gouging holes into the walls and shattering the windows. The water mains in the area were also broken and this resulted in disruptions to the water supply

A 50kg UXB from this raid, which was in reality a Delayed Action (DA) bomb, was found lying on the shingle of the North Pier extension. At 12.15pm the bomb exploded killing four soldiers of the Lancashire Fusiliers who had been standing over it and seriously injuring another. This Sunday morning raid, which was the sixth air-raid of the war on the town, resulted in 12 people being killed and a further 11 injured.

23rd October 1940: A captured Luftwaffe Dornier Do 17Z bomber was exhibited on Crown Meadow Football Ground in aid of the town's 'Spitfire Fund'. The Dornier was shot down on 15th September 1940 over Shoreham in Kent, having been severely damaged by fighters and AA fire during a daylight raid over London's Docks. The *coup de grace* was delivered by two RAF Spitfires from 609 Squadron. Three of the German crew were injured, one fatally, and witnesses who viewed the inside of the cockpit of the aircraft when it was at Lowestoft reported that bloodstains were still visible on the floor.

Dornier peep show: in October 1940 Lowestoft people had the chance to view at close quarters a fallen machine of the once vaunted Luftwaffe on Crown Meadow football ground. Even at this early stage in the war there were no doubt some who felt they had already seen too much of the enemy for their liking! (Bob Collis collection)

25th October 1940: A grim reminder that the North Sea could be equally cruel to friend and foe alike came this date with the discovery of the body of a dead Luftwaffe officer on Pakefield Beach. Oberleutnant Walter Leyerer had been the pilot of a Messerschmitt Bf 109 fighter from Luftwaffe unit 2/JG.77 which was shot down in a clash with Spitfires from 603 Squadron over the Thames Estuary during the late afternoon of Sunday 29th September 1940.

His aircraft came down in the sea and it was established that he had survived for some time in the water, for he was still wearing his life-jacket and a spent distress flare was attached to it. The body of the 30 year-old German pilot was handed over to the RAF, who also received a note from the Clerk of Lothingland District Council requesting them to fill in the necessary forms! A hint of the anti-German feeling which persisted at the time can be detected in the reply by the RAF officer concerned: *"It would be appreciated if a supply of [these] forms could be forwarded, as we hope to put them to good use in the near future."* Nevertheless, Leyerer, was buried with full RAF military honours at Ipswich on 30th October 1940. He now lies in the Soldatenfriedhof (German War Cemetery) at Cannock Chase, Staffordshire.

11th November 1940: At 2.27pm an Italian Fiat CR.42 Falco biplane fighter made a forced landing in a field close to Corton railway station. Flown by Sergete Majori (Flight Sergeant) Antonio Lazzari, aged 23, it was one of 40 fighters from the *Corpo Aero Italiano* (Italian Air Corps, an expeditionary force of the Italian Air force sent to support the Luftwaffe) flying as escort to a force of ten Fiat BR.20 bombers attempting a daylight raid on Harwich, the largest of the three raids flown by the Italians. All the Italian aircraft were flying from airfields in Belgium.

The mission was reportedly aborted due to bad weather. However, RAF Hurricane fighters from 257, 46 and 17 Squadrons intercepted the Italians over the North Sea and in the engagement which ensued, humorously dubbed 'the spaghetti party', the Italians lost three bombers and three fighters. Lazzari had a dogfight with several Hurricanes in which his CR.42 was hit in the tail. As he flew northwards his engine began to vibrate owing to a problem with the variable pitch gear of his propeller. Lazzari continued to fly low along the coast, past Pakefield cliffs and over the main street in Lowestoft, before making a forced-landing in a field just north of Corton railway station, where his aircraft went over a railway embankment tearing off the fixed undercarriage. Soldiers from the 5th Battalion, King's Own Rifle Regiment, took charge of the scene and Lazzari, who was unhurt, surrendered to a Lieutenant Way, apparently going to great lengths to impress upon his captors that he was a fighter pilot and not a bomber crewman. It is said that Lazzari was initially taken to HMS Europa, Sparrow's Nest, where he reportedly attempted to use his Italian charm on the local females employed in the NAFFI, much to the displeasure of the servicemen stationed there! Documentary evidence shows he was subsequently taken to Lowestoft Police station before being transferred to a Prisoner of War camp.

The Italian Job: surely one of the strangest visitations in WW2 was the Italian Fiat CR 42 Falco biplane fighter which force-landed in a ploughed field at Corton. Visible are .303 bullet holes in the tail unit courtesy of RAF Hurricanes. Despite being a slow biplane with an open cockpit, no radio and armed with only two machine guns, the Falco was highly manoeuvrable and often presented a difficult target for the more technically advanced RAF Spitfires and Hurricanes. (Ford Jenkins)

18th November 1940: After dropping two HE bombs on Pakefield and Oulton Broad at 9.55am, a Dornier Do 17Z circled to the west of the town. It then encountered AA shell bursts, which presumably came from a naval vessel, as no heavy guns were sited in Lowestoft at this time, and released the bulk of its 18 x 50kg bombs as it made for the coast at a height of 5,000 feet. The bombs fell in a line from St Margaret's Churchyard, across Sussex Road, Worthing Road and Royal Avenue, the last bomb landing in a minefield at North Denes. Among the casualties from this raid was ten year-old Harry Hoyle who was fatally injured by a bomb which exploded in a tree near the Ravine. Ivor Steadman from Gorleston was Harry's best friend. *"Harry and I were the best of pals. We lived close to each other in Gorleston, I lived in the High street and Harry lived in a small cottage just a short distance away. The morning after a night raid we would go out together and look for bits of bombs, shrapnel and the like to keep as souvenirs. I remember when Harry died. He had gone to see* *his father at the Sparrow's Nest, his father was in the Navy and was stationed there. Anyway there was a raid and poor Harry got caught in it. I think it was his mother who told me he had died. We all went to his funeral; he was buried in Gorleston churchyard. I'm afraid these things happened but I missed my pal."*

A soldier was also killed and 21 people were injured. Three houses were wrecked, approximately 50 more were extensively damaged and a further 200 slightly damaged in this raid, which took place without an 'Alert' having been sounded.

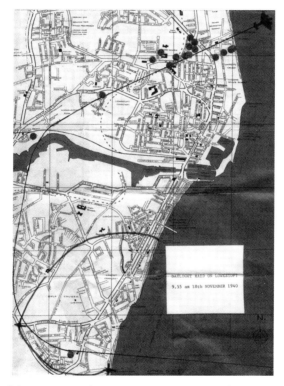

Flight path of destruction: the approximate route taken over Pakefield, Oulton Broad and Lowestoft by a single German bomber on 18th November 1940. Its bombs left two people dead and a trail of damage across the north of the town. (Bob Collis)

21st November 1940: At 3.03am the first of an eventual total of six enemy parachute mines, or 'landmines' as they came to be known, fell on the town. One fell at Pretty's Poultry Farm, Yarmouth Road and another half a mile away at the Church fields, Oulton Road. Six houses were seriously damaged and 180 more suffered minor blast effects. It was extremely fortunate that during this, or

7

later raids, none of these terror weapons, which caused widespread death and destruction in British cities, ever landed in a built up area of Lowestoft.

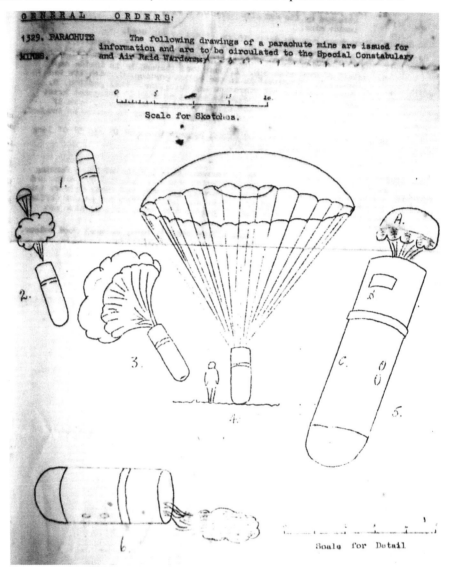

Terror weapon: this diagram, taken from a wartime Civil Defence circular, shows the size and features of the German Luftminen (aerial mine). Dropped over Britain from August 1940 they were known as parachute mines or simply 'landmines'. No fatalities resulted from the six which fell in Lowestoft but they caused severe blast damage to property over a wide area. (Bob Collis collection)

29th November 1940: A night flying Fiat B.R.20 bomber of the *Reggia Aeronautica* (Italian Air Force) based at Melsbroeck in Belgium bombed Waveney Drive at 6.39pm with 100kg HE bombs. Three bombs scored direct hits on the CWS (Co-op) Canning Factory, one exploding in the roof of the retort department causing serious damage, killing three people and injuring six more. This is believed to have been the only occasion an Italian aircraft raided the town during the War, and recent research has revealed that the three civilians who died in the raid were almost certainly the only people killed by Italian bombs in Britain in WW 2.

Mussolini's mark: recent research has revealed that the damage to the CWS factory in Waveney Drive on 29th November 1940 was the result of Italian and not German bombs. Most of the damage was caused by a 100 kg bomb which exploded in the roof of the Retort Department, fatally injuring three employees.(Ford Jenkins)

31st December 1940: The year ended with another well known landmark, the old South Pier Bandstand, being destroyed by enemy action. At 4.22pm a Junkers Ju 88 flew across the town at 1,000 feet and dropped two 250kg HE bombs. One exploded without harm in the harbour, whilst the other scored a direct hit on the pier, blasting a hole through the decking, destroying the bandstand and shattering the windows of the Pier Pavilion and 80 seafront houses and premises. Air-raid sirens were sounded, but not until several minutes after the attack! A soldier received slight injuries in the raid.

1941

The year started with a tragic case of mistaken identity, which was, sadly, to be repeated in future years. Increasingly frequent raids, often by single aircraft, destroyed and damaged many buildings in the town, some for the second or third time. Sadly the death toll continued to rise with 112 civilians and service personnel dying as a result of enemy air action.

22nd January 1941: In the first of several 'friendly fire' incidents over the town, an RAF Blenheim IV bomber, T2435 from 139 Squadron RAF, was shot down in broad daylight. The Blenheim was returning to its base at RAF Horsham St Faith (now Norwich International Airport) after a cloud-cover raid over the north German coast when, at 12.20pm, it over flew Lowestoft Harbour at 1,500 feet. Having failed to make any recognition signals, 'colours of the day', the aircraft was mistaken for a German aircraft and as a result Naval ships, which included a Norwegian paddle-steamer minesweeper, and armed trawlers including "*Lovania*" and "*River Spey*", along with guns of the recently arrived No. 158 (Light) AA Battery opening fire on it. The Blenheim was hit and crashed in flames in a field at College Farm, near Oulton Road (now Snape Drive). The crew of three, Flight Lieutenant Guy "Lemmy" Menzies DFC (pilot), a 20-year old from Christchurch, New Zealand, Sergeant. Roy Tribick (wireless operator/air gunner), aged 21 from Crewe and Sergeant.Eddie Bonney (observer), aged 27 from Bickley in Kent, were all killed in the crash.

A witness to this tragedy was Dick Wickham, then a 12 year old schoolboy, who recalls the events of that day. "*I was in a shop near our house when the AA guns suddenly opened up. It was a dull and overcast day, typical of those when hit and run raids took place. The temptation to get outside and see what was happening was too much for me, although the shopkeeper did try and stop me. As I got outside I saw the plane coming in from the sea. It passed right over me quite low, surrounded by AA fire, Suddenly the aircraft burst into flames and dived down behind the houses. There was the usual 'thump' followed by an explosion*".

Dick was certain that he recognised the aircraft as a Blenheim, even though his view had lasted but a few seconds. Despite being chastised by his mother for suggesting that British defences had shot down an RAF aircraft Dick would not be swayed from his belief, and later he was proved to be right. "*As the aircraft had crashed on fire, there seemed to be no hope for the crew. It was too low for them to bale out. An uncle of mine was in the fire service, he had to attend this crash and confirmed that it had indeed been a Blenheim. My mother apologised to me for doubting my aircraft recognition and from then, never once doubted me*"

The subsequent RAF Board of Inquiry into the tragedy highlighted a number of shortcomings in the local defences, particularly the uncoordinated manner of their operations. However, the gunners defending Lowestoft lacked any regular aircraft recognition classes and could be forgiven for being 'edgy', there had been daylight 'hit and run' attacks on the town on the 29th and 31st December 1940, and on 5th January 1941 five enemy raiders had machine gunned the town as they headed out to sea. It was also suggested that the aircraft was so badly iced up the crew were not aware they were over the coast, or that recognition signals were to be given in the area.

Victim of "friendly fire": Bob Collis with the grave of Flt Lt Guy "Lemmy" Menzies DFC, at Old Catton, Norfolk.

He and his two crewmen died when their Blenheim was accidentally shot down over the town on 22nd January 1941(Bob Collis)

4th February 1941: A Dornier Do17Z bomber from Luftwaffe unit 4/KG.2, had set out from France in clear conditions for a bombing raid against RAF Mildenhall, Suffolk, when it was intercepted and attacked by two Hurricanes from 257 (Burma) Squadron from RAF Coltishall, Norfolk. As they flew northwards across the town at 9.23am, attempting to escape the RAF fighters, the German crew jettisoned their 18 50kg HE bombs which fell in a line between the NAAFI canteen at the harbour and Compass Street, near the Town Hall. Two people were killed in St Peter's Street when two houses were destroyed by a direct hit and there was extensive damage elsewhere. The Hurricanes, flown by Pilot Officer Barnes and Sergeant Brejcha, brought down the Do 17Z which crashed in the sea off Corton killing the fluzeugfuhrer (pilot) Feldwebel Heinz Ablanski, beobachter (observer) Leutnant Friedrich Heilman and bordfunker (radio operator/gunner) Gerfreiter Fritz Muller. The fourth member of the crew, Feldwebel Waldemar Blaschyk, the aircrafts bordmekan-iker (flight engineer), survived after he parachuted into the sea. He was subsequently picked up by a Yarmouth vessel and brought ashore as a Prisoner of War.

The pilot of one of the two Hurricane fighters which intercepted the Do 17Z Sergeant Brejcha, one of the many Czech airmen who flew with the RAF, was killed four months later when the Tiger Moth he was flying crashed into the sea off Southwold in fog.

7th February 1941: A particularly memorable raid took place on this date, when at 1.08pm and without any 'Alert' having been sounded, a Heinkel He 111 flying in poor visibility at 1,000 feet came in off the sea from the east and over Lowestoft harbour. Alerted ground defences opened fire immediately and the entire bomb load from this aircraft, comprising twenty HE bombs and a few incendiary bombs, was instantly unloaded onto the Harbour Works owned by the LNER. The first few bombs fell harmlessly into the yacht basin, but one scored a direct hit on the bridge power house, demolishing it and killing the two men on duty. Another bomb fell immediately opposite on the west side of the road, narrowly missing the bridge, while the remainder left a trail of destruction across North Quay, the Harbour Master's House and Customs House being destroyed or severely damaged. The last bomb released by the He 111, a 500kg (1,100lb) weapon, fell near a railway line close to a fish siding and signal lamp room. Fortunately it failed to explode, but part of Denmark Road was closed and evacuated until it could be dealt with. One of the bombs scored a direct hit on an underground telephone centre used by the LNER Company resulting in a heavy loss of life. Ten people were killed on this date and a further 37 were injured. One of the injured died as result of their injuries two days later.

There is an interesting postscript to this raid. A 40mm Bofors gun crew from No.158 (Light) AA Battery claimed to have scored a direct hit on the He 111 with one of their shots. The following day Lowestoft Police received a report that several pieces of aircraft alloy, thought to have come from this aircraft as it headed for the sea, had been found in the East Suffolk County Council yard at Pakefield. From German Luftwaffe records, it is now known a Heinkel He 111 from unit 3/KG.53 crash-landed near Zeebrugge, Belgium after being hit by *'enemy fire'* on this date. This incident almost certainly relates to the aircraft that attacked Lowestoft, however, crew casualties, if there were any, were not recorded.

Regular updates and reports on the military situation in Great Britain were carefully distributed to neutral countries by British diplomats. Within 24 hours of the raid these reports, including a reference to the attack, were cabled to US President Franklin D Roosevelt by Lord Halifax the British Ambassador to

America. The reference to the raid on Lowestoft read; "*7. Lowestoft bombed by one aircraft p.m. February 7th. Ten workmen killed, only one naval rating wounded. Aircraft was hit and probably fell in sea*". A second reference was also made to the He 111 which had been hit by AA fire stating "*A Heinkel bomber reported shot down into the sea by anti-aircraft fire off East Coast.*"

Death from the clouds: part of the trail of destruction across the LNER Harbour works inflicted by a low-flying He 111 on 7th February 1941. Recent research suggests the raider did not escape unscathed from this bold lunchtime raid.

27th February 1941: At this time Lowestoft, along with other east coast towns and villages, suffered a period of incessant 'hit and run' attacks by Luftwaffe bombers and fighter-bombers, often flying low and using cloud cover to conceal their approach. These attacks began to take a mounting toll in lives and property. On this date Lowestoft was attacked on three separate occasions. At 11.02am five HE bombs fell in the sea off the North Pier extension, followed at 12.50pm by two heavy HE bombs in Beaconsfield Road and Lorne Park Road. At 4.02pm a final attack by a very low flying aircraft, unseen in cloud, saw bombs fall in Morton Road and London Road South. All told, 15 houses were demolished, 26 were seriously damaged and approximately 400 more suffered minor damage. Telephone wires were also brought down and the main A12 road was blocked by rubble from bomb damaged houses. Six people, ranging in age from four to 76, were killed and 19 were injured.

6th March 1941: Three daylight 'hit and run' raids took place on this date. The most damaging attack came at 12.43pm when a Dornier Do 17Z, flying at 1,000 feet through mist and light rain, approached from the east before dropping nineteen 50kg HE bombs between North Denes and Clapham Road. Among the well-known buildings added to the ever growing list of destruction through bombing were the Carnegie Free Library in Clapham Road, the School of Art, and the already damaged Technical Institute. This attack claimed the lives of three people and injured a further 23. Another attack at 4.11pm saw ten 50kg HE bombs fall across railway lines and allotments near Denmark Road. Incredibly not one of these bombs exploded and as a result Denmark Road was closed, along with Commercial Road and the Central LNER station, until Bomb Disposal Squads had dealt with the UXBs.

Carnage at the Carnegie: one of the many public buildings destroyed in 1941, the Carnegie Free Library in Clapham Road was destroyed by direct hits from HE bombs on 6th March 1941. The adjacent Technical School, already damaged by bombs a few weeks earlier, was also demolished. The Roman Catholic Church was also damaged in this raid in which three people were killed. (Ford Jenkins)

14

HMT *Evesham* (a trawler used by the Royal Naval Patrol Service) was lying beside the North Quay when it was hit by a bomb, which also failed to explode. This UXB was dealt with by a naval squad.

Dornier Do 17Z bombers (left) were responsible for a number of raids on the town. Sometimes referred to as the Fliegender Bleistift (flying pencil) it was a light bomber which in theory would be so fast it would be able to outrun defending fighters, and was popular with its pilots as a manoeuvrable low altitude light bomber capable of making surprise attacks. Despite its thin airframe making it harder to hit than other German bombers, the type proved to be the most vulnerable of the Luftwaffe's light/medium bombers and by mid 1942, had been withdrawn from service.

The Junkers Ju 88 (right) represented one of the better and more successful bomber designs to be used by the German Luftwaffe. A simple twin engine monoplane built around a pencil-like fuselage, not dissimilar to the Do 17 but with a single vertical tail, the Ju 88 proved itself as a versatile aircraft achieving success in a variety of roles. It was also the fastest bomber available to the Luftwaffe which made it ideal for 'hit and run' missions.

8th March 1941: Two Spitfires from 222 Squadron from RAF Coltishall, had just reached their patrol line over the Suffolk coast at 11.16am when a Junkers Ju 88 from Luftwaffe unit 4/KG.30 dived from clouds past the fighters, headed north across Lowestoft at 1,200 feet and dropped a stick of bombs which fell between Notley Road, Lake Lothing and the northern edge of Normanston Park. Four houses in Notley Road were destroyed and 16 people were injured but, thankfully there were no fatalities. The other bombs did little other damage apart from demolishing a cowshed and an outside lavatory!

The attacking aircraft then made for the sea and crossed out over the north of the town in the face of strong AA gunfire from No.158 Light AA Battery, and pursued by the two Spitfires being flown by Pilot Officer Klee and Sergeant

Marland. In his debrief Klee described the chase over the town as "*decidedly unpleasant as shells were bursting around us*". Minutes later the Ju 88 was brought down in the sea 6 miles off Ness Point, killing the crew of four, Hauptmann Karl Schneider, Unteroffizier, Karl Kirchner, Gerfreiter Karl Oetsch and Feldwebel Albert Ewald. Klee, was himself shot down and killed by a Ju 88 on a night sortie over Cambridgeshire two months later.

The only body recovered was that of Karl Schneider, the Ju 88's pilot. He was a very experienced bomber pilot and was a holder of the *Ritterkreuz,* Knights Cross of the Iron Cross, an award for extreme battlefield bravery or successful leadership. The fact that Schneider was not buried in the UK would suggest that his body was recovered on the German side of the North Sea.

Throughout the war 'hit and run' raids such as this often hit the wrong targets and this raid was one such instance. It is now known that the briefed target for Schneider and his crew had in fact been Newcastle!

One man and his bomb: Lowestoft Aviation Society member Phil Thacker of Carlton Colville and his unique personalised number plate ('UXB' stood for unexploded bomb in WW 2) car lend scale to a German 50kg (110lb) bomb case. The 50kg bomb was the most numerous wartime High Explosive missile dropped in Lowestoft. This inert, empty bomb casing is part of Phil's private collection of memorabilia.

1st April 1941: A German raider, again a Junkers Ju 88, was observed circling over North Lowestoft at 5.25pm by the Royal Observer Corps. Two RAF Hurricanes were climbing towards it when the German aircraft turned inland and headed towards cloud cover. However, this move did not bring the safety the crew from Luftwaffe unit 5/KG.77 had anticipated as they had failed to spot two more Hurricanes, from 242 Squadron, approaching from the south west. The RAF fighters, flown by Squadron Leader Treacy and Flying Officer Grassick, attacked the Ju 88 as it flew into the cloud. In their attempts to evade the attacking fighters the Germans jettisoned four HE bombs which landed on allotments at Oulton and Blundeston without causing serious damage. Two crewmen, Unteroffizier Werner Heidrich and Unteroffizier Klaus Petermann, the aircrafts beobachter (observer) and bordfunker (radio operator) respectively, baled out and were subsequently taken Prisoner of War. The remaining two members of the crew, fluzeugfuhrer (pilot) Leutnant Paul Meyer, and Unterof-fizier Hermann Reichmann (gunner), stayed in the aircraft and were killed when it dived into the ground at Henstead, and exploded on impact. Pieces from this aircraft, along with a more detailed account of the incident, can be viewed at the Lowestoft War Memorial Museum

9 – 10th April 1941: At 8.32pm air-raid sirens heralded the start of a night of terror for Lowestoft as ten enemy aircraft closed to carry out a 'semi-blitz' which was to be the worst the town had yet endured. The attack commenced just over an hour later at 9.45pm when a high flying raider, going east to west, dropped 300 Incendiary Bombs (IBs) most of which landed in the St Peter's Street – Beresford Road area. A few fires were started but these were all quickly extinguished. Five minutes later however, a further 300 IBs fell, and these were spread over a much wider area which included North and South Quays, Commercial Road, Denmark Road, London Road South and Kirkley Park Road. Although most of the burning incendiaries in the open were promptly dealt with, some penetrated buildings causing large fires to break out. The LNER Goods Station in Denmark Road and Social Club in Commercial Road were completely gutted.

Serious fires also took hold at the premises of Austin & Wales' Grocery, Matthew & Durrant's Garage and the County Electrical Services, all adjoining, in Clapham Road. This conflagration was no doubt the target for subsequent bomb-loads, and at 10.10pm 14 High Explosive (HE) bombs fell between Clapham Road and Suffolk Corner. Five people emerged unharmed from an Anderson shelter only four feet from a bomb crater, whilst another shelter, which was thankfully unoccupied, at the Prairie (now the site of the Britten Centre) received a direct hit. A huge 50ft x 12ft crater was blasted in Denmark Road outside the Imperial Hotel and an underground WC which was being used as a shelter was flooded after a water main burst. Of the people inside the shelter at the time only one person survived, and they had received serious injuries.

Ten more HE bombs which had fallen on the western side of town caused little material damage but had a more serious effect on sheltering civilians. A 250kg HE bomb scored a direct hit on an Anderson shelter in Rotterdam Road and nine people, seven from the same family, were killed. Six large HE bombs fell between Arnold Street and Battery Green demolishing Roberts & Son's Grocery and the nearby Morlings' Radio and Music Store. The last bombs fell at 12.30am, between St Steven's Street and Hervey Street, and here there was a miraculous escape when people in an Anderson shelter only 6ft from a bomb crater emerged with only minor injuries. The same aircraft released 200 IBs and some of these started one final blaze at Easto's Fish Curing Yard in Woolaston Road.

The 'All Clear' finally sounded at 5.25am. Some Police reports referred to the raid as a "semi-blitz", and with 46 HE bombs and 900 IBs dropped, it must have appeared that way to those in Lowestoft that night. Morale was of paramount importance, and the Police observed that *"Morale appears normal – or seemed to be the next morning"*. There was serious damage in some areas of the town, and with 20 killed and 41 injured there had been an equally heavy human toll. During the night bombs also fell at Gisleham, Carlton Colville and Bradwell.

Summarising the events of the 9-10th April 1941 Police Supt Harry Boreham wrote: *"It can be said that all services and personnel turned out promptly and did their duties very efficiently. The most gratifying feature was the fearlessness and energy with which the Incendiary Bombs were dealt with by both the trained Civil Defence staff, and the general public, even while High Explosive bombs were falling. It is reasonable to assume that, if all the Incendiary Bombs could have been got at in time, no fires would have resulted"*.

The anger at the apparent lack of defences and the frustration of not being able to hit back was not lost on Supt Boreham either. He stated that the night was clear and moonlit, but that *"There was little, if any, fire from the ground defences"*. This was because the light AA guns in the town would not have been effective against raiders above 10,000 ft, even if they had been visible.

Ordeal by fire: the view looking west across the burnt-out remains of Matthew and Durrant's Garage in Clapham Road, one of several premises fired by Incendiary Bombs in Lowestoft's worst night-raid of the war on 9-10th April 1941. The area is now the car park opposite the Library. (Ford Jenkins)

Although not part of this raid, a German Ju 88 was shot down into the sea off Lowestoft on the 9th April. The aircraft from Luftwaffe unit 11/KG.1 was missing from a night raid on Coventry and was over the sea north east of Lowestoft at 11.50pm when it was attacked by RAF fighters. The Royal Observer Corps post at Southwold reported a hostile aircraft falling in flames in the sea two miles off Lowestoft although no trace was ever found of the crew of four, Unteroffizier Kurt Neumerkel, Oberfeldwebel Fritz Rudig, Feldwebel Erich Zimmert and Feldwebel Clemens Frehe.

15th April 1941: A Royal Engineers Bomb Disposal Officer, Lieutenant I. L. Hoare, and NCO, Corporal G. W. Gibbs, were killed at 4.34pm near Arnold Street whilst attempting to defuse a 250kg HE UXB dropped in the raids of the 9th – 10th April.

Lieutenant Hoare, a 23 year-old from Norwich, had earlier set his men from 216 Section, No. 22 Bomb Disposal Company to work digging down to the bomb which had penetrated the ground near Hanby's Garage. Having reached the bomb there was a collapse of earth which almost resulted in the young officer being buried alive. Lt Hoare was rescued and taken to Lowestoft Hospital for observation and, whilst in hospital, he was visited by his section NCO, Corporal Geoffrey Gibbs, a 28 year-old from Northampton, asking for advice on dealing with the bomb. Lt Hoare promptly discharged himself and went back to work on the UXB. Exactly what happened next remains unclear but as the two men extracted the two fuses from the bomb, possibly a time-delay model, it exploded, killing them instantly.

Witnesses reported that the body of Corporal Gibbs was found in the garden of a house in a neighbouring street, having been blown over the houses by the force of the explosion. Despite an extensive search it appears that few, if any, identifiable remains of Lt Hoare were ever found. A funeral service was later held for him at Norwich Cathedral. Although there was damage to property, the entire area had been evacuated and there were no other casualties.

21st April 1941: Another night attack, this time by some seven raiders, commenced at 9.42pm with 300 IBs falling on the area between Stradbroke Road, Pakefield Street, London Road South and Walmer Road. Four large storehouses near Walmer Road were set ablaze, and two of the small but troublesome fire-bombs landed on the thatched roof of Pakefield Church. One of the bombs was successfully removed but the other had penetrated too far into the thatch and as a result, the roof and most of the Church interior was destroyed by fire.

Nothing sacred in wartime: the sad sight which greeted Pakefield residents on the morning of 22nd April 1941. AFS firemen hose down the smouldering remains of the Church, hit by just two of the hundreds of Incendiary Bombs dropped in the area the previous night. The Luftwaffe were convinced they had dealt a heavy blow to Great Yarmouth. (Ford Jenkins).

Once again fires acted as a beacon for other German bombers in the area, and the focus of this attack now became South Lowestoft and Pakefield, where more HEs and IBs rained down. Within minutes two HE bomb loads fell between Grayson Drive and Cliftonville Road, and in the Walmer Road – Wellington Road area. In Stradbroke Road a Mr and Mrs King spent an eventful night in their garden Anderson shelter. Aware that bombs had fallen in the vicinity they were surprised to find their exit from the shelter was jammed. When they were freed at daylight the next morning they discovered how lucky they had been, for a 250kg UXB had fallen next to their shelter, churning up the ground and blocking their exit. They had in fact spent the night with an unexploded bomb buried only a few feet from their shelter!

The largest stick of bombs to fall that night, twelve in number, fell at 10.17pm in a cluster at the junction of Kirkley Park Road and London Road South, near the Marlborough Hotel. There was a lucky escape when a large HE bomb blasted a huge 40ft x 20ft crater in the grounds of St Mary's Convent School. St Luke's Hospital, which was used by the Royal Navy, suffered considerable window damage, but the affected area was thankfully unoccupied. Even the dead were not allowed to rest in peace as a large HE bomb fell amongst graves on the Western edge of Kirkley Cemetery and 300 IBs were scattered over the same area.

The final stick of bombs fell between Elm Tree Road and Long Road at 10.40pm. By this time a heavy sea mist was fortuitously rolling in over the area, and it is widely believed by many people that this prevented the enemy from carrying out an even more punishing attack on the town.

When the 'All Clear' finally sounded at 11.18pm, 25 houses had been destroyed or seriously damaged, gas and water mains were broken and telephone lines had been brought down. Hundreds more homes had received minor damage from blast or IBs. Three people were killed and 21 injured – a surprisingly low casualty figure considering the number of bombs dropped, 46 HEs and an estimated 1,000 IBs.

In an interesting tailpiece a German Luftwaffe appraisal of their raids on 21st April 1941 recounted that several crews reported seeing *"Five large fires started in the vicinity of the docks at Great Yarmouth"*. It is now known that no bombs were dropped on Yarmouth that night and the 'large fires' the Luftwaffe crews reported were almost certainly those in Pakefield.

A night to remember: men from the Pakefield Auxiliary Fire Service (AFS) station standing with the 250Kg bomb which blocked the entrance to an Anderson shelter in Stradbroke Road. The shelter is just visible to the right of the picture. The man in the boiler suit (4th from left) is Herbert 'Rufus' Hadenham, who had his own miraculous escape from unexploded bombs on 14th March 1945 when two crashed through a farm building where he was working after a USAAF B-17 Fortress crashed near his farm at Carlton Colville. (Bob Collis collection)

2nd May 1941: In another damaging night raid 19 HE bombs fell on LNER Harbour Works, causing serious damage to workshops, railway lines and sidings in the same area that had been attacked on the 7th February. An hour later more HE bombs fell amongst anti-tank blocks at Oulton then, at 11.38pm, two parachute mines drifted down to explode near Gorleston Road, where both left craters over 40ft in diameter, the blasts shaking the town. When the final toll of damage was taken 15 homes had been wrecked, 40 more seriously damaged and 200 others damaged to some degree. Two people were killed and 13 injured. Despite this, the morale of the public in the area of this serious incident was described by the local police as being "*very good*".

3 – 4th May 1941: Between 11.06pm and 12.36am five Luftwaffe aircraft attacked Lowestoft, causing widespread serious damage. One of the first bombs in this raid fell in Police Station Road – on the very same spot where another HE bomb had landed three months earlier! The now battered Police Station and Report Centre were seriously damaged and had to be evacuated, and some of the houses and businesses in north Lowestoft affected by this raid were damaged for a second or third time. A delayed action HE bomb in the cellar of a house in Old Nelson Street exploded nine hours later, adding to the damage. Four large HE bombs fell at College Farm, Oulton Road but did little damage, but a bomb with a delayed action fuse meant a sudden surprise explosion six hours later.

At 12.17am a stick of bombs fell near Blinco Road in Oulton Broad. Most were small and a few IBs were also scattered among them. Almost 12 hours later, at 11.17am, a 250kg delayed action bomb went off, making a crater 30ft x 12ft and partly demolishing seven bungalows.

Finally at 12.36am two parachute mines were dropped. One landed on the sea wall north of the Gasworks and the blast was terrific. Such was the force of the explosion it not only damaged the windows and roofs of over 450 houses and businesses, it also detonated 15 landmines on the beach and North Denes. The second parachute mine landed in the water at Waveney Dock where it failed to explode. The Royal Navy were hurriedly evacuating their ship and shore personnel, when at 5.30am the mine detonated underwater. Two mine sweepers, one of which was HMT *Ben Gairn*, were sunk, the Trawl Market was damaged and approximately seven people were injured.

5th May 1941: For the third night running, the town was the target for German bombers. The first of three attacks commenced at 12.08am with the dropping of two HE bombs, one of which sank a blockship in the mouth of the harbour, the other embedding itself in the decking of the South Pier without exploding. The second attack had altogether more serious consequences for some well known businesses, when ten HE bombs and a few IBs fell between Stanley Street and the Marina. Fish curing premises, the Eastern Counties Omnibus garage and a laundry at The Prarie (now the Britten Centre) were all seriously damaged. A serious fire broke out at Woolworths in London Road North which the AFS finally brought under control at 2.35am, but by then both Woolworths and the adjoining Timpsons were totally burnt out. The last attack of the night saw 18 x 0kg bombs falling in the sea off Kirkley Cliffs, causing damage to the windows of nearby hotels and boarding houses.

Remarkably, there were no reports of any injuries in the aftermath of this attack. This was partly explained by the Police who stated that the houses in the area affected had either been closed altogether or the occupants went out of town at night to sleep.

From the ashes of despair: the charred remains of Woolworths, ("Woolies") following the night raid of 4-5th May 1941. It is believed an oil Incendiary Bomb caused the fire which destroyed the popular London Road North store. The shop was rebuilt on the same spot and it was only in 2009 that a world-wide recession finally resulted in the closure of these well-known premises. (Ford Jenkins)

11th May 1941: Lowestoft was one of five coastal locations, which included Southwold and Aldeburgh, to be strafed by Messerschmitt Bf 109s, resulting in two minor casualties and *"Slight damage at all these places"*. It would appear the Germans were chased by RAF Hurricanes from 257 (Burma) Squadron from RAF Coltishall, although they evidently failed to get within firing range as there were no claims by 257 Squadron on this date.

12th May 1941: Yet more damage was inflicted to LNER lines, sidings and railway trucks near Commercial Road as four heavy HE bombs fell from one of the raiders which attacked in the early hours at 2.28am.
 Six people died and 15 were injured in the rubble of their own homes as an HE bomb demolished four houses and badly damaged 74 more in the May Road area.

19th May 1941: On this date some retribution was exacted for the damage the Luftwaffe was inflicting on the town. At 12.07pm a Messerschmitt Me 110 fighter-bomber, from the unit I/SKG.210 based at Merville in Normandy, France, emerged from cloud and headed north across the town through a hail of AA gunfire to drop two HE bombs. One landed in Pickling Plots near the Gasworks, detonating some landmines, whilst the other fell on shingle at the North Pier Extension and failed to explode.

Shot down over Lowestoft: German pilot Hans Hasse described the barrage which greeted his Me 110 as it flew across Lowestoft on 19th May 1941 as "A Hell of fire". This artist's impression by John Reeve shows Hasse's aircraft bursting into flames after repeated AA hits to the engines. Its bombs caused only minor damage and the aircraft crashed in the sea. The German pilot was picked up and brought to Lowestoft, but no trace was ever found of his observer. (Reproduced courtesy John Reeve)

24

Hit by ground fire, the Me 110 burst into flames before crashing in the sea off Corton. A patrol boat which reached the scene 45 minutes later picked up the pilot, 20 year-old Lt Hans "Ulli" Hasse, who was brought ashore and became a 'guest' at Lowestoft Police Station.

In May 1977 the ex Luftwaffe pilot, then living in South West Africa, marked the anniversary of the shoot down and his survival by sending a telegram to the town: it simply read "Best Wishes". His escape from the blazing aircraft after it hit the sea was indeed fortunate; no trace was ever found of his crewman, Unteroffizier Wilhelm Neumann, who was, in Hasse's opinion, already dead when the aircraft hit the water.

Cream of the Luftwaffe: 20 year old Hans "Ulli" Hasse (left) was already a veteran before his war ended in the skies over Lowestoft on 19th May 1941. In this portrait picture, he wears the uniform and insignia of a Leutnant, and an Iron Cross first class. Badges worn include pilot's wings, Luftwaffe eagle and a gold war flight badge (awarded for 50+ operations). He had already flown 56 operations against Britain as a Ju 88 pilot with KG.4 before he joined a new unit, SKG.210, with their Me 110s. In May 1977, to mark the anniversary of his "visit" to Lowestoft.

Herr Hasse (right, photographed in 1977) sent a telegram to the Mayor of Lowestoft from his home in Tsumeb, SW Africa, now Namibia. (Bob Collis)

26th May 1941: Ten people were killed and eleven injured in a senselessly destructive attack at 6.40pm. A Do 17Z which had been flying at about 4,000ft circled the town several times before AA guns opened up with "*vigorous fire*". After diving to about 1,500ft to release two heavy HE bombs, the raider continued out to sea apparently undamaged. One of the bombs practically demolished a row of terrace houses in Wood's Loke with a 20ft deep crater replacing the spot where Numbers 5 and 6 had stood. The other bomb fell on allotments causing a massive crater some 50ft in diameter.

Battered but defiant: by May 1941, London Road North had been hit by bombs on six separate occasions and a considerable number of shops and premises were beyond economical repair. Records show that, during the war, there were a total of 9,433 individual reports of damage to property in Lowestoft. (Ford Jenkins)

4th June 1941: People living in Tonning Street had a lucky escape when a huge 1,000kg (2,200lb) HE bomb fell near the Eagle Tavern at 12.40am, but failed to explode. Houses within a 100 yard radius were evacuated, but an elderly lady asleep in one woke up to find her neighbours gone and the area cordoned off and deserted! The UXB was safely defused by members of No.22 Bomb Disposal Company, Royal Engineers. Other bombs in Whapload Road and Old Nelson Street did, however, cause serious damage to property, killing a sailor and injuring five more.

Hermann the German: the largest bomb dropped on Lowestoft by the Luftwaffe in WW2 was the SC1000 or 1,000kg HE bomb, named "Hermann" after their similarly well-proportioned Commander-in-Chief, Hermann Goering. At least two of these huge bombs are known to have fallen without exploding. This is the example which fell in Tonning Street on 4th June 1941 being recovered by a Royal Engineer's Bomb Disposal Squad. Without mechanical plant, excavating unexploded bombs could be a long and arduous process. In this case the local police had to wait five days until Lieutenant Collier, the officer in charge of the disposal operation, issued a clearance certificate. (Ford Jenkins)

13th June 1941: At 3.45am a lone bomber approached from the south at 2,000ft and dropped seven HE bombs between the Trawl Basin and Whapload Road. One sank a blockship, others wrecked Naval offices and damaged the new brick-built Naval canteen. The last two bombs penetrated and exploded inside the Central School, demolishing the centre and completely wrecking the remainder. Like many schools and public buildings, the Central School had been requisitioned as billets for the large number of military personnel in the town, and at the time of the raid a number of soldiers had been asleep in the building, consequently there was a dreadful toll in lives; 14 men, principally from the Royal Scots and Royal Engineers, were killed. Of the six seriously injured soldiers one died two days later.

14th July 1941: Within the space of 24 hours, two RAF Wellington bombers came down in the sea near the town. The first, X9634/AA-V, an aircraft from 75 (NZ) Squadron at RAF Feltwell, Norfolk, suffered an engine failure whilst climbing at 6,000ft over the Suffolk coast en route for a night raid on Bremen. The pilot immediately turned about but was unable to maintain height and the Wellington crashed into the sea off Corton. Despite being injured, the two pilots, Pilot Officer F. T. Minikin and Sergeant Gilding, managed to escape and were picked up by a Naval craft at 2.15am before being taken to Lowestoft Hospital. Sadly the other members of the crew were not so lucky; Sergeant E Fox, Sergeant F. J. E Price, Pilot Officer J. T Leacock and Sergeant H. P Clarkson all perished.

By a rather bizarre coincidence, the two sets of propellers from this aircraft were recovered separately by fishing boats exactly ten years apart, one in 1977, the other in 1987.

This photo shows No. 30 Course, 11 Operational Training Unit at RAF Bassingbourn, Cambridgeshire. Circled are; Sgt Gilding, 2nd row far right, P/O Leacock, third row 6th from left, Sgt Clarkson, front row 6th from left and Sgt Fox, front row 2nd from right, some of the crew members of Wellington X9634. Of the four, only Sgt Gilding survived. Interestingly, this photograph was taken around June/July 1941. Given X9634 crashed on the 14th July 1941 the crew members in this photograph were probably on one of their first sorties (via Ken Flavell)

28

The following night the Royal Observer Corps reported that an aircraft had exploded in the air and fallen in flames into the sea several miles off Pakefield. This was Wellington R1614/BU-H from 214 Squadron, which had taken off from RAF Stradishall, Suffolk, at 11.15pm, also heading for a night raid on Bremen. Tragically, all six on board, Pilot Officer V. K Brown, Flight Sergeant W. G Lewis, Sergeant R. D Hull, Sergeant M. R Collins (RCAF), Sergeant J. Taylor and Sergeant J. S Else, were killed.

Local people later bore witness to the vagaries of the tides which brought the parachute and harness from the pilot, Pilot Officer Brown, ashore at Pakefield, while his body was recovered on the German occupied Dutch side of the North Sea, where he was buried in the Bergen-opp-Zoom War Cemetery. The bodies of Flight Sergeant Lewis and Sergeant Hull were washed ashore on English beaches but the remainder of the crew were never found and, as such, their names appear on the Air Forces Memorial to the missing at Runnymede. BU-H was one of two 214 squadron aircraft lost on this night.

The sea gives up its dead: Pilot Officer Vic Brown was the pilot of the Wellington which exploded over the sea off Pakefield whilst outbound on 15th July 1941.
His body was recovered and buried by the Germans on the Dutch side of the North Sea.
A strange twist of time and tide saw his parachute harness washed up at Pakefield. (via Bob Collis)

22nd July 1941: At 1.06am South Lowestoft bore the brunt of a particularly nasty attack. Wartime press reports referred to this raid as having been carried out *"at rooftop height"* and the fact that the four heavy HE bombs fell in a cluster close to the junction of St Leonard's Road and Lorne Park Road tends to bear this out, although it would have been unusual for a night raid. Three bombs scored direct hits on houses in the closely built up area and in total 20 houses were also totally destroyed. In addition 30 houses were damaged beyond repair, 50 seriously damaged and close to 300 houses and shops less badly hit. The Police recorded that 15 Anderson air-raid shelters were also involved in this incident; 13 survived intact, one was damaged and one was destroyed – the latter being empty at the time. Despite this, it now appears that 13 people were killed, several in Morrison shelters in their homes.

Three of the dead were sailors from HMS Europa who had been billeted in houses which were destroyed. Two of these sailors have their names recorded on the Royal Naval Patrol Service (RNPS) memorial in Belle Vue Park and are listed as having "no known grave".

Total devastation: Naval personnel help with clearance work after four bombs from a low-flying raider blasted 20 houses around the junction of St Leonard's Road and Lorne Park Road into rubble in the early hours of 22nd July 1941. (Ford Jenkins)

10th August 1941: The Royal Observer Corps reported four enemy aircraft passing over during the night, and at 1.03am four HE bombs fell from one of these between Raglan Street and Trafalgar Street, wrecking 10 houses and damaging many others. One of the bombs landed directly between two Anderson shelters at the rear of Woolaston Road, destroying both and killing all six occupants. One of the casualties was 17 year-old RAF Apprentice William "Sonny" Powell. He had been home on leave and was sheltering with his parents, both of whom died with him in this tragedy.

Battery Green Rd
September 4th. 2 houses demolished also a warehouse.
6 houses, 8 industrial buildings, 2 shops, 1 church and
1 cinema damaged.

Beach Rd
September 4th 6 houses and 1 office damaged.

Beaconsfield Rd
October 3rd. 2 houses wrecked, and 6 shops, and
31 houses damaged.
1943 September 8th 2 houses demolished and 1 shop and 4
houses damaged.

Beccles Rd
September 4th 7 houses damaged.

Counting the cost: the keeping of diaries, or notes, relating to enemy action was officially frowned upon. However, young Peter Killby defied the authorities and compiled his own survey of visible damage, occasionally updating it as the war progressed. The result was an extraordinary list of damaged properties covering most of Lowestoft, stark proof if it was ever needed, of the bombing ordeal suffered by Britain's most easterly town. (Bob Collis)

1942

The number of raids began to reduce this year though 1942 started with the now infamous 'Wallers Raid' on 13th January when 71 people died. As the year progressed so did the raids claiming the lives of another 23 people.

13th January 1942: Lowestoft had by now experienced many raids in which the damage and casualties had been grievous, but the events of this day would make it the blackest in the town's wartime history. An 'Alert' had been sounded at 4.20pm and snow was falling when seven minutes later, from out of the cloud to the south, came a lone Dornier Do 217 from Luftwaffe unit 9/KG.2 based in Holland. The aircraft, following the line of the main street, dropped four large HE bombs on the main shopping area in London Road North, and in a matter of seconds almost a whole row of shops and premises were blasted into piles of rubble.

Waller's Restaurant (where most of the casualties occurred) and the premises of Boots, Fifty Shilling Tailors, Morlings', Bonsalls', Freeman Hardy & Willis and Davis' Dental Surgery were all destroyed. Rescue teams, reinforced by parties from Eye, Ipswich, Pakefield, Saxmundham and Woodbridge, toiled frantically in freezing conditions for four days to clear the rubble and extricate survivors and, incredibly, twelve people were pulled from the debris alive. A soldier received the George Medal and two members of the Rescue Party were awarded the British Empire Medal for their work at this incident. Possibly the saddest story was that of a 17 year-old girl who was found after 48 hours buried in the cellar beneath the mountains of rubble which had been Waller's Restaurant. Tragically she died shortly after reaching hospital. Despite there being many stories of miraculous escapes, the casualty list was nothing short of horrific; 71 (52 civilians and 19 service personnel) were killed and over 150 were injured, 41 of these seriously.

On the 11th February 1942 Major Selwyn W Humphrey, Mayor and ARP Sub-Controller for Lowestoft, reported to the Town Council on two letters from opposite ends of the social scale which had been received in the aftermath of this terrible raid; one was from HM The Queen, notifying despatch of a quantity of blankets and tea *"for the distressed"*, the other came from a 9 year-old boy who enclosed 2s 5d (about 12p today) in stamps *"For the bombed-out people of Lowestoft"*.

Despite the pain and suffering endured by the people of Lowestoft they remained steadfast. This is borne out by two entries in the Police summaries made at the time, *"Although the casualties at Lowestoft after the raid of 13th January were the heaviest yet encountered, there was no evidence of undue panic"*.

Horror in the snow: the view looking down London Road North in the after-math of Lowestoft's worst raid of the war on 13th January 1942. Several of the town's best-known shops, including Boots the Chemist and Freeman, Hardy and Willis were among those destroyed. (Ford Jenkins)

"Damage at an East Coast Town": this was all the heavily censored wartime newspapers could carry by way of a picture caption following the infamous "Waller's raid" on 13th January 1942. Both the Marina Theatre in the back-ground and the Odeon the opposite side of the street (now W. H Smiths) were utilised as temporary mortuaries when a heavy death-toll became evident. The area pictured is now a car park behind Waterstones book shop and Savers. (Ford Jenkins)

Another stated *"Recent raids on Lowestoft do not appear to have increased evacuation to any extent"*

This was the worst single air-raid incident in East Anglia in WW2 and passed into local folklore as "The Waller's Raid". In January 1992, on the 50th anniversary of the raid, the Jack Rose Old Lowestoft Society unveiled a memorial plaque to the victims of this and other attacks on the town in the shopping precinct. Today the plaque resides at the Marina.

It was also in 1992 that the German pilot responsible, Oberleutnant Ernst Walbaum, who was at the time of the raid Staffelkapitan (Squadron CO) of 9/KG.2, was identified from German records. He was killed, together with two other crewmen when their Do 217 crashed at Zandvoort in Holland whilst on a training flight on 22nd March 1942. It also became apparent the crew believed the town they had hit had been "Fischmarkt", the German code name for Great Yarmouth.

Did it really happen here ?: Few of the busy shoppers passing the area today have any inkling of the death and destruction which occurred on this spot that snowy afternoon in 1942. A plaque commemorating these and all the other Lowestoft air-raid victims was erected by the Jack Rose Old Lowestoft Society in 1992 and is now located on the North wall of the 'Savers' shop, close to where the bombs fell. (Simon Baker)

23rd January 1942: Just ten days after the devastation wrought in Lowestoft's main street another serious raid occurred. The 'Alert' sounded at 8.42am and a minute later a Junkers Ju 88 came roaring out of the snow clouds which had once again gathered over the town, diving in the direction of the main LNER station, which appeared to be its target. If so, the four HE bombs it dropped missed and blasted 21 houses in Summer Road and Stanley Street into heaps of rubble. ARP and Rescue Party personnel who reached the scene were horrified to find amidst the debris a coffin containing a corpse. The funeral of the deceased was to have taken place that day and mourners were among the victims – 12 people were killed and 14 injured, ten of these seriously. Utility services were also affected when a four inch water main was fractured.

By this time the AA gunners from No. 43 AA Brigade had heavy AA gun sites located in the town and several of these engaged the raider, despite the bad weather. One of the Bofors gun crews claimed a hit on the Ju 88, but records show no German aircraft were lost over the UK on that date.

29th May 1942: Another "friendly fire" incident with tragic consequences occurred on this date. At 7.15pm a Beaufighter VIF, T4919/ND-B from 236 (Coastal) Squadron, stationed at RAF Wattisham, Suffolk was returning from a patrol off the Dutch coast when it was mistakenly attacked by two RAF Spitfires from 610 Squadron. The Spitfires, based at RAF Ludham, Norfolk, had been sent to investigate the Beaufighter after it had been plotted as a "*suspected hostile*" aircraft. The Exact circumstances that led to the events that followed remain unclear, but the Spitfires engaged and opened fire on the Beaufighter, which crash-landed with its port engine on fire in a field at Gisleham.

During the crash the aircraft struck an anti-invasion cable seriously injuring the observer, Sergeant S. Walker, and trapping him in the burning aircraft. He was freed from the wreckage and rushed to Lowestoft hospital, but died as a result of his injuries later the same day. Surprisingly, the subsequent RAF Court of Inquiry partly blamed the Beaufighter pilot, Pilot Officer S. B. Ash, who survived the incident, for taking evasive action when engaged by the Spitfires and therefore "*behaving like a hostile aircraft*"!

5th June 1942: Kimberley Road in South Lowestoft had already suffered from enemy action in 1916 when a bomb from a German Zeppelin shattered many windows. Twenty six years later the German Luftwaffe returned to continue the assault. At 1.22am four heavy HE bombs fell, three in Kimberley Road and one in nearby Waveney Crescent. A sad quirk of fate resulted in a child being rescued unhurt from a Morrison shelter under the wreckage of a demolished house, while both parents, who had been sleeping beside the shelter, were killed. Five houses were completely demolished by the bombs, one of which made a crater 50ft in diameter.

5th July 1942: The body of a German airman, 28 year old Oberfeldwebel Paul Krause, was washed ashore at Pakefield. Research has revealed that Krause was the bordfunker (radio operator) aboard a Heinkel He 111 bomber from unit Erpr.u.Lehr Kdo 17 which was en route for Nuneaton on the night of 24-25th June when it was attacked over the North Sea by an RAF Mosquito night-fighter. As a result of the Mosquito attack flares ignited inside the fuselage and Krause, believing the aircraft was going down, bailed out. In fact the damaged Heinkel managed to limp back to its base, where, after landing, the crew found their comrade was missing.

Nicht Zurucken (Failed to return): Luftwaffe radio operator Paul Krause baled out over the sea off the Suffolk coast after an encounter with an RAF Mosquito night-fighter on 25-26th June 1942. His three crewmen managed to fly their damaged He 111 back to base at Chartres, where Krause was found to be missing. (Simon Baker)

30th July 1942: In July 1941, two RAF Wellingtons had come down in the sea off Lowestoft within 24 hours of each other. On this occasion, a year later, the aircraft were German.

During the night of 29-30th July, German aircraft withdrawing from a raid on Birmingham crossed East Anglia and several were destroyed by the British defences. A Mosquito night-fighter from 151 Squadron at RAF Wittering, Cambs intercepted a Dornier Do 217E-4, Werk-Nr.5469 U5+GV, from unit 11/KG.2 which was heading for home at 14,000 ft. Cannon and machine-gun fire from the Mosquito sent the Do 217 diving into the sea with both engines and the fuselage in flames. In their de-brief the RAF crew reported seeing: "..*a body or a dinghy fell away from the e/a* [enemy aircraft] *during the dive*". On 7th August 1942, the body of a crewman from the Do 217, Unteroffizier Wilhelm Elbers, the bordmekaniker (flight engineer) was found on a sandbank three and a half miles off Lowestoft. His body was recovered and brought ashore for burial in Lowestoft Cemetery.

The following night the Luftwaffe again struck at Birmingham, and more of the raiders flew across the eastern counties at low-level in an attempt to avoid the British defences on their way home. At 03:23 on 31st July, a German aircraft was sighted flying low over Lowestoft in a south easterly direction and *"emitting showers of sparks from both engines"*. From Luftwaffe records it is now known that Do 217E-4 Werk-Nr.5427 U5+IR, from unit 7/KG.2, was lost over the North Sea that night. The body of one crewman was eventually washed ashore in Denmark, but no trace of the other crew members was found.

19th October 1942: Between 6.53am and 9.24pm there were continuous intermittent air-raid 'Alerts' as some 35 hostile aircraft made daylight cloud-cover raids over East Anglia in poor visibility. At 8.50am a Junkers Ju 88 from Luftwaffe unit 4/KG.6 flew north across the town at 500ft and was engaged by Lewis Machine Gun (LMG) fire from the ground defences. It appears the pilot was hit and the Ju 88 dived into the ground amid anti-tank defences at the Church Fields (now the junction of Spashett Road/Crestview Drive) 100 yards from the perimeter of 478 Battery Heavy AA gun site H2, where it exploded on impact and burst into flames. Five minutes later another explosion in the burning wreckage, possibly a 250kg HE bomb detonating, injured an Army officer who had run across to the crash from the AA site in a vain search for survivors.

The day Lowestoft hit back: a fire hose plays on the smouldering wreckage of the Ju 88 shot down in the Church Fields on the morning of 19th October 1942. The diagonal lines in the background and around the wheel hub were made by the wartime censor in an attempt to delete the "anti-invasion defences" - in reality steel scaffolding poles - from the picture. The nose of an unexploded 250kg bomb can be seen protruding from the side of a ditch in the foreground, two others exploded in the crash and subsequent fire. The crew were all killed. (via Ian McLachlan)

The remains of the four German airmen, Leutnant Dr Wilhelm Blackert (pilot), Unteroffizier Alfred Bohnemann (observer), Unteroffizier Helmut Mollenhauer (radio operator) and Feldwebelw Meinhard Smit (gunner), were recovered and subsequently buried in a group grave in Lowestoft Cemetery. Although several aircraft were hit over Lowestoft, this was the only raider brought down in the town in WW2. Small pieces of the Ju 88, recovered at the time as souvenirs, can be seen on display at the Lowestoft War Memorial Museum at Sparrow's Nest.

They fell for the Fuhrer: two headstones, each bearing two names, mark the last resting place of the four men comprising the crew of the Ju 88 which crashed in Lowestoft on 19th October 1942. Initially only one name and one identity disk could be found amongst the wreckage to identify the crew. It was only after the war that the (then) Imperial War Graves Commission was able to identify the crew from captured German records and place the names of the four Luftwaffe men on the grave. (Simon Baker)

6th November 1942: A cloud-hopping Dornier Do 217 dived across Oulton Broad and released four heavy HE bombs at 1.08pm. Swannell's Maltings were extensively damaged by a direct hit and part of one building collapsed into the Broad. One bomb blew a crater 48ft in diameter in a slipway at Leo A. Robinson's boatyard and a Motor Gun Boat (MGB) under repair there was wrecked. Another bomb fell in the water nearby killing hundreds of fish which were gratefully picked up by local fishermen. There was a narrow escape when one of the bombs landed only 60ft from a building used to store naval torpedo warheads and other explosives. One man was seriously injured in this raid and despite the efforts to save him he later died in hospital. Two RAF Typhoon fighters attempted to intercept the German raider but it managed to escape.

Broadside bomb-site: Swannell's Maltings were badly damaged by a direct hit from an HE bomb on 6th November 1942, and part of the building collapsed into the Broad. The raiding Do 217 escaped. (Ford Jenkins)

6th December 1942: An RAF Boston aircraft from 88 Squadron made a forced landing in a field at Brew House Farm, Carlton Colville at 1.50pm. The aircraft, flown by Sergeant Chas Tyler, was returning home on one engine to RAF Oulton, near Attleborough in Norfolk, from 'Operation Oyster', a daylight raid on the Philips radio and valve factories at Eindhoven, Holland.

Sergeant Bob Gallup, the aircrafts observer, recalls the incident: *"Shortly after we had released the bombs we were hit by flak in the starboard engine. We lost contact with the rest of the Squadron as we began to slow down. We were unable to gain height and the prospect of covering the 150 mile North Sea return flight looked remote, so it was decided to force land in Holland and give ourselves up. After turning back inland however, we conferred once more and decided to 'have another go'. We turned for the Dutch coast once more and as we crossed out again every gun in Holland seemed to be firing at us. The tracers seemed to be like hailstones in reverse. Over the sea we tried to gain a little height but were unable to do so. After about 50 minutes we recognised Lowestoft ahead.*

We crossed the coast and force landed immediately, finishing wheels up in a ploughed field at Carlton Colville. My feet were buried in soil and I had a problem getting out through the top escape hatch. As we hit the ground the strap of Chas Tyler's seat harness broke and he hit his head on the gun sight. Apart from that we were unhurt. Chas was taken to Lowestoft hospital while Stuart [Sergeant I. Stuart the aircraft's wireless operator and air gunner] and I were taken home for a lovely meal by the farmer. After we had been to see Chas in hospital, we were taken to the local pub where we were allowed to win every game of darts! We spent the night at the farm near the aircraft, with clean sheets and pillows. Life was great until next morning when transport arrived to take us back to camp."

Operation Oyster was, at the time, the largest daylight raid staged by No.2 Group Bomber Command, and came with a high cost. The raid was planned for a Sunday to reduce civilian casualties. However, some 148 people were killed. Of the 93 aircraft that took part in the raid (47 Venturas, 36 Bostons and 10 Mosquitoes) 14 (9 Venturas, 4 Bostons and 1 Mosquito) were lost, some 15% of the force. Many of the returning aircraft were damaged to some extent or another – 23 by bird strikes!

On a wing and a prayer: the RAF Boston bomber which returned from the bold daylight raid on Eindhoven on one engine on 6th December 1942 and force-landed in a field at Carlton Colville. Two of the crew were "entertained" in a local pub while the pilot received treatment in Lowestoft Hospital for head injuries received in the crash. (Pavel Vancata)

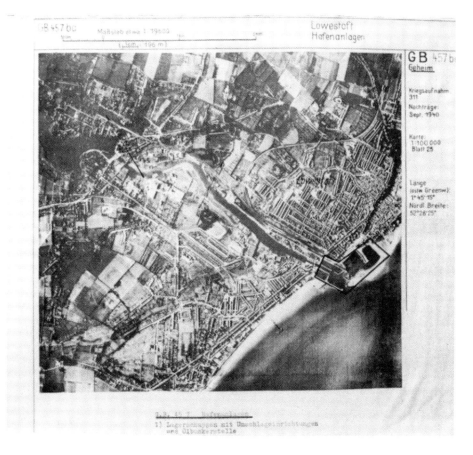

Through German eyes: This picture, taken in September 1940, and used in a Luftwaffe target folder, shows how interested the Luftwaffe were in military activity in the port. Intermittent reconnaissance sorties over the town continued right up until November 1944 (Via Chris Elliott)

1943

Though there was a continued reduction in the number of raids during 1943, the year bore witness to a surprise attack which, despite only lasting literally a matter of seconds, was one of the worst of the War, second only to the previous years 'Waller's Raid'.

11th January 1943: On this cold and cloudy day a drizzly rain had started to fall when, at 12.01pm, a Junkers Ju 88 from Luftwaffe unit KG.6, based in Holland, headed across Lake Lothing from the south west. Flying at 1,000ft, the raider released 11 HE bombs, all of which exploded harmlessly in marshy ground and water to the east of the Silk Works, then occupied by the Royal Navy with HMS Myloden, a Landing Craft, Tank training unit. As the Ju 88 headed over Lowestoft, making for home, it flew through a terrific barrage of AA gunfire from the 3.7inch guns of site LH 3, Light AA units and considerable 20mm cannon fire from Naval vessels in the dock. The guns continued firing as the Ju 88 went out to sea, and it was with satisfaction that a report was later received that the raider had been crippled by this intense ground fire and had come down 2½ miles from shore. There were no survivors.

It had been a particularly successful day for the defences as a second Ju 88 was hit over Yarmouth at about the same time and also went into the freezing waters of the North Sea with the loss of the crew. Both of these losses were confirmed in Luftwaffe records.

18th March 1943: A night raid aimed at Norwich and Yarmouth by 20 German bombers saw a number of incidents in the Lowestoft district. At 11.04pm a mixed load of IBs including 50kg phosphorous bombs, combined with 50kg HE/IBs (*Sprengbrand C50*)to the Germans, "Firepots" to the British ARP personnel) and normal IBs fell between Laurel Farm, Oulton and Woods Loke. A straw stack and a shed were set ablaze and the resulting fire appeared to attract more bombs. A minute later 120 1kg IBs, some with steel noses and some with an explosive charge under the tail, showered down on an area 600 yards x 300 yards including Princes Road, Water Lane, Oulton Road and St Margaret's Road. Seven of the fire bombs hit St Margaret's Church but fortunately the damage was very slight. The same aircraft dropped "firepots" on southern Lowestoft, and one started a serious fire at the Pickfords furniture depository in St John's Road, which was gutted by the ensuing blaze.

Other bombs fell in the area at Fritton and Hopton. Raid spotter Edwin Comber recorded that the glare of fires burning and the flashes of heavy AA gunfire from batteries in Lowestoft were visible from his Observation Post at Bracondale in Norwich! Incredibly, given the ferocity of the attack and the concentration of bombs, there were no casualties.

"Firebomb Fritz": this was the name given to the German Brandbomben (Incendiary Bombs) in wartime propaganda posters. The small (16 inches long) but troublesome incendiaries known to the Germans as the B1E1, were dropped on Britain by the thousand.
It is estimated that some 18,000 fell in the Lowestoft district, 10,000 of them in one raid in 1943. Although many fell in open ground and others failed to ignite, they caused considerable damage to property in some incidents.
(Bob Collis)

11th May 1943: At 11.23pm a searchlight on Lowestoft seafront illuminated a Luftwaffe Dornier Do 217E-4 bomber flying at very low level and approaching from the east. It is not known whether the pilot was blinded by the glare of the searchlight beam, or if he attempted to evade it, but the aircraft crashed into the sea just 300 yards off Ness Point, killing the crew. The aircraft, U5+FL from unit 3/KG2, had been despatched on a mine laying mission off Cromer and was one of four lost on operations against Britain that night. Its pilot, 23 year-old Leutnant Eberhard Pleiss, was flying his first operational sortie.

Nineteen days later, on 30th May 1943, the body of an unidentified German airman was washed up on the beach at Gunton. No identity discs or papers were found on the body, but his uniform was that of a Leutnant. He was buried in grave No. 522 at Lowestoft cemetery on 2nd June 1943, his headstone bearing the legend 'Ein Deutscher Soldat' (A German Serviceman). Almost a month later, on 29th June 1943, the body of a Luftwaffe NCO was washed up on Lowestoft's North Beach. His identity disc bore the Number 57359/227 and the Germans identified the airman as Unteroffizier Wilheim Stocker, the beobachter (observer) aboard DO 217 E-4 U5+FL. He too was buried in Lowestoft cemetery. The two other crewmembers onboard, Obergefreiter Carl Busch (radio operator) and Oberfeldwebel Hermann Heuyng (gunner) were never foun

The first and the last: Eberhard Pleiss was typical of the young German aircrew flying on the western front with the Luftwaffe in 1943. His first operational flight, a mine-laying operation off the East Coast, proved to be his last. His father, a fighter pilot with the Imperial German Air Service in the 1914-18 war, queried whether his son had received enough training. (Bob Collis collection)

Although to this day still formally unidentified, it is widely believed that the body washed ashore at Gunton was that of the young Eberhard Pleiss, a belief that is shared by Eberhard's sisters who visited Lowestoft Cemetery on 11th May 1993, the 50th anniversary of the loss of their brother's Do 217.

Known unto God: "Ein Deutscher Soldat" (A German Serviceman) are the words inscribed on the headstone of the unidentified Luftwaffe Leutnant buried in Grave 522 at Lowestoft Cemetery. Could this be the last resting place of Eberhard Pleiss? (Simon Baker)

12th May 1943: The first of two devastating low-level attacks on Lowestoft was launched at 8.41am by Focke-Wulf FW 190 fighter-bombers from Luft-waffe unit II/SKG.10, based in Belgium. Six aircraft attempted to bomb two trawlers used for training by the RNPS about half a mile offshore.

Their bombs missed, but cannon and machine gun fire caused casualties amongst the ships crews. One of the FW 190s then headed inland and dropped a single 500kg HE bomb which bounced 150 yards from gardens at Belle Vue Park onto houses in Royal Avenue before exploding. Three houses were com-pletely demolished and over 100 more damaged. Five people were killed and a further 12 were injured, ten of these seriously.

Further FW 190's were sighted flying at 800ft some 55 miles east of Lowestoft. These were turned back and chased by RAF Spitfires.

Later that evening, at 9.00pm, a larger force of 24 FW 190s came roaring in over the Lighthouse in North Lowestoft heading south, firing their guns and releasing their bombs at rooftop height.

Although the attack lasted less than 20 seconds it was, in terms of damage, the most destructive the town had experienced. Sadly, the Royal Observer Corps post on Corton Road had spotted the incoming FW 190s, but was unable to raise the alarm as the cable connecting the post with the 'Crash' air-raid alert had been severed in the morning attack. Police reports state that 21 500kg bombs fell on or near the town.

Of these two fell in the trawl basin, three in the sea north of the Claremont Pier, one in the outer harbour and two failed to explode. There was another narrow escape when a UXB fell only 26 feet from a gasholder in Whapload Road before bouncing into a brick wall and breaking up.

The other bombs left a trail of death and destruction across the town at the following locations: Norfolk Street (two killed); Alexandra Road; the quay at Waveney Dock; Corton Road (three killed) – this bomb also destroyed the new Rescue Party Depot in Lyndhurst Road; Ipswich Road; High Street where three bombs fell, one was a direct hit on the "*Jubilee Stores*" Public House where a 21st birthday party was being held (16 killed) and started a serious fire at Watson's Garage, destroying several Army vehicles; Raglan Street (three killed); Whapload Road (one killed) and Wildes Score, this bomb virtually demolished Wilde's School which at the time was the HQ of the Lowestoft ATC unit.

Richard Reeve remembers the attack. "*Before the war my family lived on Somerleyton Road, Oulton, but by 1942 my mother, sister and I were living in Norwich, my father was serving with the Royal Engineers. My grandmother lived at 28 St Margaret's Road and we would visit her sometimes, the stays coinciding with my father's periods of leave. I recall being shocked by the damage that Lowestoft had suffered, particularly in the High Street. I also remember travelling on buses with black curtains draped over the windows. When there was an air raid we had the option of using the Morrison shelter, which doubled as a table in the living room, or the Anderson shelter in the back yard. I remember frequent trips to both when the siren sounded. However, one evening I was awoken by a great commotion and my uncle, who slept in the same room as me, came bounding up the stairs and rushed to the window. I got up and stood there with him when, with an almighty flash and sound of explosion, the whole room lit up. A minute afterwards my mother came up and admonished us both, but particularly Uncle Bob, for standing at the window during a raid! The next morning we found out that the explosion was Watson's Garage being hit. Despite the garage being just around the corner in the High Street and the tremendous explosion my grandmother's windows, which were taped up remained intact!"*

The party's over: local legend has it that a 21st birthday party for an RNPS sailor was underway at the Jubilee Stores when the FW 190s struck at 9.00pm on 12th May 1943. A 500kg bomb completely destroyed the pub, killing 16 of the occupants. Watson's Garage, opposite, was set ablaze by the same bomb. The pub was never rebuilt. (Via Steve Snelling/Archant)

46

Three of the FW 190s swept on down the coast to attack Kessingland, where the village blacksmith was killed by gunfire within yards of his home at 'Ivy Nook'. The Germans also destroyed the blacksmith's shop and three adjacent houses at an area known locally as 'Blacksmith's Corner' with their bombs, before sweeping back out to sea.

Day of the Jabos: the Germans referred to these low-level attacks by FW 190s as Jabo angrieff (fighter-bomber raids). This is the terrifying sight which roared low over the rooftops in Lowestoft at 9.00pm on 12th May 1943. Although it lasted only a matter of seconds, the raid that evening caused heavy damage and one of the worst casualty lists of the war. (via Bob Collis)

The damage inflicted on Lowestoft was of a very heavy scale with 51 houses and premises demolished, 90 very seriously damaged, 225 extensively damaged and some 700 with minor damage. Rescue parties from Eye, Ipswich, Saxmundham and Woodbridge again assisted with rescue work. Casualties in this sudden unexpected attack were similarly heavy; 32 people were killed and 51 injured, a death toll exceeded only by the 'Waller's Raid' on 13th January 1942.

The following day the Police reported that the conduct of the general public in Lowestoft after this last daylight raid was *"very good"*.

In the aftermath of the destruction wrought by the FW190s on 12th May, Lowestoft was visited by General (later Sir) Frederick Pile, Commander in Chief of Britain's Anti-Aircraft defences. In an attempt to deter further low-level attacks 12 RAF barrage balloons were sited in the town. They arrived on the morning of the 15th May 1943, and it proved to be fine timing as another FW 190 raid had been planned for Lowestoft that same night. At 10.00pm a force of 15 fighter-bombers (again from II/SKG.10) approached the town, only to find their way barred by balloon cables. Frustrated at being unable to hit their intended target the German pilots headed south and attacked other Suffolk coastal locations including Wangford, Southwold, where ten people were killed, and Felixstowe. One of the raiders was shot down by an RAF Typhoon flown by Richard Hough from No.195 Squadron based at RAF Ludham, Norfolk. Hough himself was lucky to return to Ludham. Believing to have been attacked from astern by another unseen FW190, he had in fact been hit by a 20mm shell, which exploded in his radio compartment, from a British vessel offshore which had been firing at the FW190's!

A UXB from this raid hit the headlines in 2008 after it was 'misplaced' by a Royal Navy Explosive Ordnance Disposal team. The bomb, which had been recovered from Felixstowe beach, was eventually located and blown up.

From Germany with love: this 20 mm shell case was found on the roof of a cycle shed near the Eastern Coach Works by Mr Charles Holt the day after the low-level raid. Hundreds of similar cases were found scattered along the flight-path of the raiders, a grim confirmation that they used cannon and machine-gun fire to add to the destruction. At least two people are known to have been killed by gunfire from the FW 190s. (Bob Collis)

23rd October 1943: The RAF estimated that some 18 German bombers were operating this night. Their target was Yarmouth, but the raid went badly astray. At 11.15pm German aircraft approaching from the east and north-east began crossing the coast between Lowestoft and Gorleston and over the next 35 minutes a spectacular stream of coloured flares, about 70 in total (9 fell unexploded) were dropped by raiders attempting to find their target. It appears that five straw stacks were set ablaze by IBs at Corton, where seven IB containers were found, and these fires, combined with those at the "Starfish" fire decoy site at Lound, caused the majority of the raiders to drop their loads in open country. A further 13 IB containers were discovered in the grounds of the Golden Sands Holiday Camp and five more in the vicinity of Rogerson Hall. The only serious damage in the Lowestoft area was at Oulton where a nurses' home was destroyed by fire. The Police also recorded that large numbers of IBs and some HE bombs fell in the sea off Corton Beach. It was subsequently estimated that 37 HE bombs (two of which were unexploded) and some 8-10,000 IBs had fallen, in all some 34 tons of bombs, which had for the most part fallen harmlessly in fields at Corton, Oulton, Hopton, Flixton, Lound and Blundeston. Some IBs at Gorleston were the nearest bombs to the target that night. Incredibly there was only one casualty, a soldier seriously injured by a falling IB at Corton.One of the most bizarre items dropped on Britain by the Luftwaffe fell at Oulton that night. Some 2,000 Caltrops or "Crowsfeet" fell from a container across Gorleston Road and a number of ARP or NFS vehicle had their tyres punctured by the small four pointed steel stars. These odd devices had presumably been intended to either fall on Allied airfields, or more likely their intended target, where they would have retarded the use of emergency vehicles en route to fires etc Searchlight units were busy and heavy AA gun sites expended 1,563 rounds of ammunition that night with some success. German records confirmed that two bombers crashed in the North Sea with the loss of all their crews whilst three others crashed on their return.

Aerial oddity: among of the strangest objects dropped by the Luftwaffe over Lowestoft were the four-pointed steel stars known as caltrops or "crowsfeet". Intended to puncture the tyres of vehicles, or aircraft if dropped on airfields, about 2,000 were dropped by container in the Gorleston Road area at Oulton during the eventful night of 23rd October 1943. (Bob Collis)

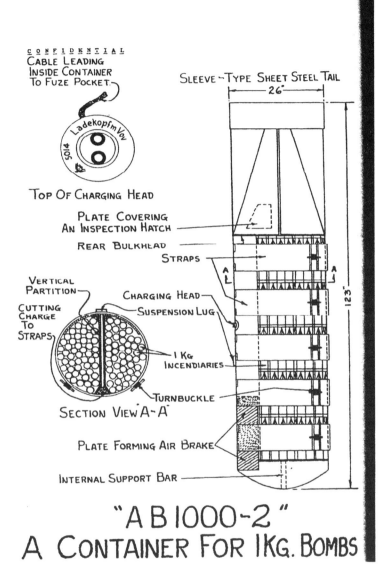

CABLE LEADING
INSIDE CONTAINER
TO FUZE POCKET

Ladekopfm Vov
5014

TOP OF CHARGING HEAD

PLATE COVERING
AN INSPECTION HATCH

REAR BULKHEAD

STRAPS

SLEEVE — TYPE SHEET STEEL TAIL
26"

A

123"

VERTICAL
PARTITION

CUTTING
CHARGE
TO
STRAPS

CHARGING HEAD

SUSPENSION LUG

1 KG
INCENDIARIES

TURNBUCKLE

SECTION VIEW A-A

PLATE FORMING AIR BRAKE

INTERNAL SUPPORT BAR

"AB 1000-2"
A CONTAINER FOR 1KG. BOMBS

How it works: Diagram from an Army Bomb Disposal manual showing the German AB 1000-2 container, the biggest of the so-called "Hermann's bread basket" fire-bomb carrying weapons. Each AB 1000-2 could hold up to 720 Incendiary Bombs. Set to open at low altitude, the container could lay an unprecedented concentration of bombs in a small area, causing very serious problems for the NFS and ARP services. (via Patrick Rushmere)

1944

With the Luftwaffe all but beaten, their ability to launch raids was severely diminished. Indeed the last raid by a manned German aircraft took place in April 1944, however, that did not signal an end to enemy attacks from the air. As the year progressed the Germans changed their tactics, and the Vergeltungswaffen eins, revenge weapon 1 or V-1 made its first appearance, starting a new phase of fear and suffering. Another noticeable change was the large numbers of Allied aircraft, particularly American, over the town as they set off on daylight raids to the heart of Germany. With this came an increase in the numbers of aircraft crashing in the Lowestoft area, all too often, with a tragic loss of life.

4th February 1944: In January 1944 the Luftwaffe launched its final offensive against Britain. Code-named "Operation Steinbock", here it became known as "The Baby Blitz" and, whilst the principal target was London, bombs were often scattered over a wide area of south east England. At 4.40am two large AB1000-2 Incendiary Bomb containers, the largest of their kind dropped on Britain by the Luftwaffe in WW 2, fell on allotment gardens, one either side of Gunton St Peter's Avenue in Wardens sector No.21. The containers did not open in the air and their contents, a total of 1,188 1kg IBs burned out in two small craters. Nobody was hurt.

It happened one night: looking more like a garden ornament than enemy action, this is the sight which greeted one Walmer Road resident after a German AB 1000-2 Incendiary Bomb container disgorged its contents in the vicinity before falling to earth at 00.25 on the night of 23rd February 1944 during the "Baby Blitz".
(via Bob Collis)

6th March 1944: A USAAF B-24 Liberator bomber, 42-64457 from the 733rd Bomb Squadron, 453rd Bomb Group, based at Old Buckenham, Norfolk, was returning from the American 8th Air Force's first large scale daylight raid on Berlin when it came down in the sea three miles off Corton at 3.52pm. The aircraft, one of 216 despatched on this raid, had suffered serious flak damage over the target and was then attacked by enemy fighters on the return journey. As the B-24 approached the coast the crew started to abandon it, and witnesses on the shore reported seeing four parachutes descending from the aircraft before it hit the sea. Motor torpedo boats from Lowestoft and Gorleston were quickly on the scene, with minesweepers and an RAF Walrus aircraft also assisting in the search. Of the crew of ten, five were rescued and one body, that of Technical Sergeant Trall W. Wertz (gunner), was recovered from the sea. The remaining four members of the crew, 2nd Lieutenant David D. Wallace (co-pilot), Staff Sergeant Floyd R. Rogers (engineer), Technical Sergeant Robert B. Williams (gunner) and Staff Sergeant Godfrey B. Suter (gunner) were never found.

On this date the USAAF 8th Air Force lost a staggering total of 60 B-17 Fortress and B-24 Liberator bombers on the Berlin mission. While losses were heavy, the Allies could replace men and machines fairly quickly. The German Luftwaffe, however, was now in decline and in the months ahead its fighter force was steadily decimated in the air and on the ground by Allied long-range fighters and bombing raids.

T/Sgt Trall W. Wertz. the 27 year old from Pennsylvania had been a replacement crew member on B-24 42-64457 and was the only casualty recovered after it ditched in the North Sea off Lowestoft. Wertz (who's mother was born in Germany but emigrated to the USA when she was 16) was temporarily interred at the American Military Cemetery at Madingley, Cambridgeshire, before being repatriated to the United States in July 1948, when he was laid to rest in the Arlington National Cemetery. (USAAF)

27th March 1944: An RAF Air Sea Rescue launch had the sad task of landing at Lowestoft the bodies of five Allied airmen (three RAF(VR), one RAAF and one RNZAF), who were killed when their aircraft crashed in the sea. All had been crewmen aboard a Halifax bomber from No.192 (Special Duties) Squadron based at RAF Foulsham in Norfolk. On the night of 26th March the aircraft had set out on a Radio Countermeasures (RCM) sortie in support of a large force attacking Essen. After an SOS was picked up from the bomber, it crashed into the sea 60 miles off Cromer killing the crew of eight.

9th April 1944: At 9.45pm the body of a USAAF P-47 Thunderbolt fighter pilot from the 56th Fighter Group at Boxted was brought ashore at Lowestoft. 2nd Lieutenant Arlington Ward de Canizares Jr, a 22 year-old from Wayne, Philadelphia, was killed when his aircraft went down in the sea 20 miles off Lowestoft. He had been part of a three aircraft flight escorting a bomber mission to Posen, Germany, and had already had a successful combat with enemy fighters in which his flight claimed one destroyed, one 'probable' and one damaged.

During the return flight they were attacked from astern by another German fighter, and de Canizares, despite being out of ammunition and extremely low on fuel, turned into the attack to enable his fellow pilots, Major Schreiber and Lieutenant J McClure, to engage. The enemy fighter was driven off but de Canizares' P-47 ran out of fuel as a result of his brave action. Left with no option but to bale out he climbed out of his aircraft, but was knocked unconscious after striking the tail unit as he fell. An RAF Air Sea Rescue launch picked up the badly injured de Canizares but he failed to regain consciousness and died shortly afterwards.

American hero: 'Ward' De Canizares' selfless act of bravery during a bomber escort mission ultimately led to the young USAAF Thunderbolt pilot losing his life over the sea off Lowestoft on 9th April 1944.
(Holton Airfield Memorial Museum)

In a letter to de Canizares' mother, Major Lucian A Dade Jr of the 56th Fighter Group wrote: *"You must realise that Ward gave his life so that all you folks back home, plus the rest of us overseas, can one day return to a normal and happy life. Knowing Ward as I did, I know that he accepted this gamble as part of the game- and that when the end came, he died as he would have wanted to – flying".*

21st April 1944: The last raid by a piloted German aircraft on the Lowestoft area took place at 1.25am when a Messerschmitt Me 410 dropped eight 50kg HE bombs between Chestnut Avenue and the LNER sleeper depot on the edge of Lake Lothing. A house on Normanston Drive, near Oulton Broad North Station, was partly demolished and a woman was treated for shock. It was estimated that there had been 70 German aircraft operating on this night and the principle target for this force was Hull. Interestingly, not one bomb fell there!

22nd April 1944: At 10.00pm on this Saturday night a large number of USAAF B-24 Liberator bombers were returning in darkness from a late afternoon mission to Hamm, Germany. The American crews, few of whom had night-flying experience, were crossing in with their navigation lights on when they were attacked by a small number of Me 410 Intruder aircraft which had followed them in over the coast. In the ensuing 40 minutes of chaos nine Liberators were shot down over Suffolk and Norfolk and several more were destroyed as they attempted to land. Over 60 USAAF airmen were killed. Two aircraft from the 448th Bomb Group, based at Seething, were shot down in flames by the Me 410s near Lowestoft; one crashed in the sea a mile off Hopton at 10.07pm with the loss of all 10 crew, the other crashed, minus its tail unit, at 10.20pm on marshland at Kessingland, killing the crew, 2nd Lieutenant Eugene. V. Pulcipher (pilot), 2nd Lieutenant Elmer. P. Meier (co-pilot), 2nd Lieutenant William Carcelli (bombardier), Staff Sergeant Chester. J. Romanosky (radio operator), Staff Sergeant. James. R. Hardin (gunner), Sergeant William. H. Durrant (gunner), Sergaent William. S. Davis (gunner), Sergeant Maynard. H. Young (gunner) and Sergeant Carl. E. Spellman (gunner). Two Me 410s were lost.

Gordon Jermy was on duty in the Royal Observer Corps post at Pakefield (D4/14) that evening and recalls *"I can remember how angry I was at so little being done to warn the USAAF crews that the enemy were in their midst. I reported to our ROC centre in Bury St Edmunds that I believed I had a hostile night-fighter overhead of Pakefield Post, a perfect silhouette against a dusk sky. The Liberators continued pouring out an assortment of coloured flares and within minutes of my report, short, sharp bursts of enemy cannon-fire started ripping the Lib's apart. From our post, which had a perfect 360 degree visibility, I recorded 12-14 Lib's shot down, but there was so much to report to our HQ that the details ran into each other".*

On 22nd April 2010, 66 years after the crash, a ceremony was held at Kessingland's St Edmunds Church to dedicate a memorial stone honouring the crew of B-24 843 'Repulser'. The service, which was attended by over 200 people, was led by the Rt Rev Graham James, Bishop of Norwich, and Canon Lyndy Domoney, Rector of Kessingland. United States Air Force personnel from RAF Mildenhall formed an Honour Guard.

Beautiful but deadly: From 1943 one of the most memorable sights in the sky over Lowestoft was the assembling groups of USAAF heavy bombers on their great air offensive against Nazi Germany. By February 1945 it was frequently possible to count up to 1,000 B-17Flying Fortresses (pictured) and B-24 Liberators as they set out. Vere McCarty, a B-24 Liberator Bombardier with the 446th Bomb Group at Flixton, recalled "I remember Lowestoft – at least as it appeared from the air. It was a very welcome view to see, coming home across the North Sea from its' not so welcome side". (USAF via Martin Bowman)

30th May 1944: USAAF B-24H Liberator, 42-52739 *"Red Growler"*, from the 838th BS, 487th BG at Lavenham, Suffolk, was returning from a daylight raid over Munster, Germany with flak damage when, at 1.00pm, it came down in the sea off Lowestoft. The pilots managed to successfully ditch the aircraft in one piece near several small fishing boats, but it sank within 3 minutes of hitting the water. The radio operator managed to release two life rafts and nine airmen were rescued by members of the Royal Naval Patrol Service within twenty minutes of their going into the water. Sadly one of the gunners, Staff Sergeant Julian W Messerly, was unable to inflate his 'Mae West' life preserver, and was last seen clinging to the tail of the bomber as it sank, the other crewmen having been unable to reach him. He was never found.

1st July 1944: The first German V-1 Flying Bomb, or 'Doodlebug' as they became known, was reported over the area. At 7.43pm the Royal Observer Corps posts at Southwold and Wrentham plotted a V-1 going NNE over Southwold at 2,000 feet. It crossed out over Covehithe, and shortly afterwards an explosion was heard as it fell into the sea off Kessingland.

Thousands of these small, pulsejet-powered missiles, each carrying a 1 ton HE warhead, were launched towards London during this period from sites in France. The small number which completely overshot into East Anglia had suffered a failure of their air-log counter, which caused them to fly on until their fuel was exhausted. The first in Suffolk had fallen at Peasenhall on 16th June 1944. On 12th July East Suffolk Police reported: "*Large numbers of people are coming into the area from London and the surrounding districts subjected to this form of bombing. Judging from their demeanour it appears to shake morale more than the bombs dropped by enemy aircraft.*"

6th July 1944: At 8.17pm an unusual incident occurred when an aircraft identified by the Royal Observer Corps as a USAAF P-47 Thunderbolt fighter accidentally fired its guns while flying west across the town. One of the .5 calibre rounds penetrated a house in Long Road, where it knocked a hole three inches square through the wall plaster. The bullet was removed from the premises by Police Inspector Read, and it was very fortunate that the occupant, a Mrs Evans, was unharmed.

5th August 1944: A USAAF B-24 Liberator from the 489th BG based at Holton (Halesworth) was returning at 3.10pm from a daylight raid over Brunswick, Germany with flak damage when it came down in the sea three miles off Lowestoft. The crew of ten all parachuted into the water, nine were rescued by RAF Air Sea Rescue (ASR) launches and one by a local fishing boat. The American airmen were brought ashore at Lowestoft and Yarmouth.

16th September 1944: The men on duty at the Lowestoft Royal Observer Corps post witnessed an unusual, and possibly unique, event when at 7.29am, they reported sighting "*a large spiral column of smoke, with a red flame behind it, going up to the E.*" Conditions were clear that morning and the column of smoke, headed by a missile which they reported *"looked like a cigar"*, was seen to curve over and fall towards London. What they had seen was in fact the 16th German V-2 Long Range Rocket being launched towards London from the Dutch island of Walcheren. It is now known that the rocket fell on Southgate, killing six people. Although no V-2s fell on Lowestoft one did fall at Hopton on 3rd October 1944, and it was frequently possible on clear mornings and evenings to see the vapour trails left by the climbing rockets, over 100 miles away, on their 5 minute journey to England. Later research has established that Lowestoft had indeed been fortunate to escape the terror and destruction of these weapons as the town was in fact included on a list of targets for the rockets.

29th September 1944: An RAF Mosquito XIX, MM643 RS-F, from 157 Squadron stationed at RAF Swannington, Norfolk was taking part in a daylight air sea search with an RAF Air Sea Rescue launch, for another Mosquito and crew from the same squadron which had failed to return from an "Intruder" sortie during the night.

At 11.11am, whilst over the North Sea off Lowestoft, the Mosquito was attacked by enemy aircraft and shot down. Both crew members, Flight Lieutenant S. A. Waddington and Flying Officer E. H Lomas, were killed. The crew of the missing Mosquito, Flying Officers Fry and Smith, were killed having being shot down over Holland.

11th October 1944: The first damage inflicted on Lowestoft by a V-1 Flying Bomb occurred at 4.40am, when a V-1 was hit by AA gunfire as it approached from the NNE at an altitude of 800 feet and exploded about 500 yards offshore. Thankfully, there were no reports of casualties but the windows of 18 houses and shops were damaged by the blast.

All the V-1s which crossed the area during this period were launched at night from points off the east coast by specially adapted Heinkel He 111 bombers from Luftwaffe unit III/KG.53, based in north Germany. Their target was London. The Germans switched to this method of launching V-1s as a result of the Allied advance overrunning the launch sites in France. The British defences were redeployed to meet the new threat and this included the installation of Heavy AA gun batteries at Pakefield and Hopton, in what became known as the "DIVER Strip", 'DIVER' being the code word for the V-1. The shells fired by these guns were equipped with new proximity fuses and the guns themselves used American built gun laying radar which made them particularly successful, in fact it is recorded that 26 V-1s were hit causing them to explode in the sea off Lowestoft.

Deadly offspring: converted Heinkel He 111 bombers were used as "mother" aircraft to air launch V-1 Flying Bombs towards London from over the North Sea at night during the autumn and winter of 1944-45, and Lowestoft was often on their flight path. Out of some 9,000 V-1 Flying Bombs sent towards the UK between 13th June 1944 and 29th March 1945 only 17 examples either failed to explode or part exploded. Of the 1,200 v-1s launched by He 111s only 638 functioned properly and a mere 66 – about one in every 20 launched – reached their target, London. (picture courtesy the late Frank Leyland)

14th October 1944: This proved to be a most eventful night as a wave of V-1s began approaching the Suffolk coast at 8.00pm and two minutes later Lowestoft had another scrape with disaster. A V-1 which was heading towards the coast at Corton cut out as guns opened fire on it. Observers on the ground held their breath and waited for the bang but, incredibly, the V-1 glided for almost two miles across north Lowestoft before finally exploding in the water of Lake Lothing, in the Inner Harbour. The explosion brought 255 separate reports of damage, principally to windows, and included several buildings, Roman Hill and Gorleston Road Schools among them, located more than a mile from the impact site!

At 8.05pm a V-1 received a direct hit from AA fire and exploded over South-wold. Blast from the warhead rocked the town and damaged some 565 proper-ties, including some at Reydon. Another V-1 hit by gunfire over the coast fell to earth in a hedgerow at Back Road, Hopton. The missile was badly damaged but the warhead failed to explode. The following morning tragedy struck as three Royal Engineers Bomb Disposal Squad officers were examining the wreckage. A fuse pocket found amid the wreckage exploded as it was being examined, killing one of the officers, Lieutenant C J Bassett, and injuring the other two. By a bizarre coincidence another wrecked but unexploded example fell only three quarters a mile away on 10th December 1944. This time the Bomb Disposal team took no chances; the fuse pockets were gathered up, placed in the small crater made by the crashing missile, and blown up in situ.

19th October 1944: About eight V-1s crossed the Suffolk Coast during the night. At 5.10am a V-1 which had been hit by AA gunfire over Lowestoft crashed into treetops 100 feet from Mancroft Towers, a large house in Oulton Broad. The missile exploded above the ground and Mancroft Towers was severely damaged by the blast wave. Three other houses sustained extensive damage but no casualties were reported. The vivid flash and the explosion of this V-1 were seen and felt some ten miles away in Beccles.

Blasted by a "Doodlebug": Mancroft Towers, one of the largest private houses in Oulton Broad, narrowly escaped destruction on 19th October 1944. A V-1 skimmed over the building and detonated in treetops nearby, the blast-wave causing extensive damage which took many months of work to repair. (via Bob Collis)

4th November 1944: At 2.40pm a USAAF P-51D Mustang fighter, 44-13860 *"The Roller"*, from the 339th Fighter Group at Fowlmere in Cambridgeshire made a forced-landing on Manor Farm Marshes at Kessingland after running short of fuel whilst returning from operations over Germany.

As a result of the forced-landing the undercarriage collapsed and the propeller was damaged but the pilot, Flight Officer Leo Henry Becker, escaped unhurt. The only 'casualty' from the incident was reported to have been a pheasant which failed to become airborne fast enough and was killed when struck by the Mustang's tail.

The war rolls on: the only 'casualty' was a bird which failed to outrun Lt Becker's USAAF P-51D Mustang fighter "The Roller" as it force-landed through shortage of fuel on marshes at Kessingland on 4th November 1944. (John Harris, 20th Fighter Group Association)

8th November 1944: At 9.50pm a Mosquito B.IV from 1655 Mosquito Training Unit (MTU) at RAF Wyton crashed and burst into flames near Oak Farm, Lound, killing the crew, Flight Lieutenant Clancey and Flying Officer Alford MiD. The Mosquito had been on a night cross-country exercise and it is thought the pilot lost control whilst making a course change, sending the aircraft diving into the ground. As an illustration of how the war dealt bitter blows to some families, two brothers of Flt Lt Clancey, the Mosquito's pilot, were lost while serving in the Army; one was posted missing in North Africa in November 1941, while the second was killed during the Rhineland offensive in March 1945.

9th November 1944: USAAF B-17 Flying Fortress bomber 42-102931, *"FIKLEBITCH"*, of the 452nd BG from Deopham Green, Norfolk was seen circling over Lowestoft at 7.30am with an engine on fire. The aircraft was part of a formation assembling in the area for a daylight mission to attack marshalling yards at Saarbrucken in Germany. Eventually the burning engine fell from the B-17 and landed on waste ground in London Road North, on the site of what had been Waller's Restaurant, which had itself been destroyed by bombing in 1942. A bomb bay door also fell from the stricken bomber and landed in the garden of 17 Sussex Road. The blazing aircraft headed out to sea before crashing two miles north east of the town. Four parachutes were seen descending and a search of the area was made by rescue craft, but the North Sea again proved fickle and of the crew of nine comprising, 2nd Lieutenant Francis W Meyers (pilot), 2nd Lieutenant Fred Prado (co-pilot), 2nd Lieutenant Robert L. Hester (navigator), Staff Sergeant Aldo Valenzano (bombardier), Staff Sergeant Robert M. Long (radio operator), Staff Sergeant Donald E. Turman (gunner), Staff Sergeant Jackson C. Britt (gunner), Staff Sergeant Albert R. Richards (gunner) and Technical Sergeant Harold DeYoung (engineer) only the body of the pilot (Meyers) was found, still attached to his parachute.

During the evening a high flying German Arado Ar 234 jet reconnaissance aircraft over flew the town. This was the first occasion, according to the Ministry of Home Security, that a manned hostile German aircraft had crossed the British coast since August 1944, and it was almost certainly the last piloted German aircraft to over fly Lowestoft in WW2. Coincidentally, the first enemy aircraft over the area, on 17th October 1939, had also been on a reconnaissance sortie.

14th November 1944:   Another tragic "friendly fire" incident occurred this date when at 7.12pm an RAF Mosquito NF XVII night-fighter, which had inadvertently pursued a V-1 Flying Bomb into a coastal gun belt, was brought down in flames by Heavy AA guns, crashing at Decoy Farm, Blundeston. The Mosquito, which came from 68 Squadron at RAF Coltishall, was crewed by two US Navy Officers, Lieutenant Joseph Francis Black and Lieutenant Tomas Newkirk Aiken, who were part of a group of personnel attached to the RAF squadron to gain experience in night-fighter techniques. This exercise proved to be a costly one for the Americans; out of the group of ten volunteers who arrived in the UK, six (including Black and Aiken) were killed on operations. The gun crews on the Suffolk coast had strict instructions regarding the identification of any aircraft approaching the 'DIVER Strip'. Sadly, the inexperienced American crew, probably being too intent on catching the V-1, did not follow the laid-down procedures to identify themselves and, as a result, were fired upon. Recent research has shown that the V-1 the two men died pursuing got through the British defences and fell near Berkhampstead, Hertfordshire. Fortunately there were no casualties.

A memorial to the two men was unveiled by Lord Somerleyton (then aged 16) in 1944, and can still be seen beside a bridleway at the Warren, close to the spot where their aircraft fell to the earth. On the 60th anniversary of the tragedy, Sunday 14th November 2004, a service of remembrance was held at the memorial and attended by nearly 50 people, including personnel from the US Air Force based at RAF Mildenhall.

Many of the night-fighters were assisted in their nocturnal hunt for V-1 carrying Heinkel He 111s by the cliff top RAF Chain Home Extra Low (CHEL) radar station at Hopton, north of Lowestoft. This station was built in 1940 in an attempt to 'plug the gaps' in the main British Chain Home radar network coverage, which could only see and track aircraft down to 500ft. As the war progressed improved equipment enabled RAF Hopton to vector fighters onto very low-flying enemy raiders as far afield as the Dutch coast. The RAF maintained an intermittent presence at the site right up until the 1990s, when it was finally sold. The current owners, Frank and Gail Brown, have landscaped parts of the site but are keen to preserve this piece of local military history, and, as such, have made no attempt to interfere with the Cold-War underground installation or the concrete pads on which the WW2 radar towers once stood.

19th November 1944: Several V-1's approached or passed over the area this night. At 7.57pm a V-1 which had reportedly been damaged by AA fire (although Lowestoft Police did not report any gunfire) cut out over the town going in a westerly direction. Forty-five seconds later it fell to earth with a tremendous explosion at Low Farm Cottages, Carlton Colville.

Richard Reeve remembers hearing the distinctive sound of the V-1 as it approached. *"I was in my grandmother's garden in St Margaret's Road when I heard the familiar sound of a V-1 'Buzz Bomb'. As it passed overhead the engine cut out and I shot indoors and jumped under the Morrison shelter. My grandmother said I had done the right thing but if it cut out overhead you were safe as it would continue gliding for a while. I later found out it came down at Carlton Colville."*

The explosion blew a 37 feet crater in the clay soil and this soon filled with water. Two cottages were demolished and two women occupying one of these, Agnes Grimble and Edith Ribbans, were killed instantly, their dog however survived and was later dug out of the debris. The couple who occupied the other cottage, Mr and Mrs Lew Paul, returned home from a visit to the cinema in Lowestoft to find their home destroyed. A further six houses were severely damaged, ten received extensive damage and 80 *'minor'* damage from the blast. Sixteen people were injured, one of them seriously. This incident was the worst involving a V-1 in the district and the resulting casualties were the last caused by enemy air action in the Lowestoft area in WW2.

There but for the grace of God go we: Mr and Mrs Lew Paul survey the wreckage of their home at Carlton Colville, flattened by a V-1 which exploded near Low Farm Cottages, claiming the lives of their neighbours while Mr and Mrs Paul were at the cinema in Lowestoft on 19th November 1944. Many houses in the area were affected by the terrific blast-wave. (Jeff Gorrod)

Not surprisingly by now a degree of 'war-weariness' was beginning to manifest itself. Suffolk Police *reported "There is a certain amount of nervousness on the part of the public towards Flying Bombs. This is more apparent when they are flying low and the public appear to regard them with much more apprehension than a raid by aeroplanes".* The report went on to state *"There is a certain amount of alarm, especially among older people".*

The Other Side

BERLIN   Number 2

HOW MUCH LONGER WILL IT LAST?

WHEN is this bloody war going to end? You over there prob_ ably ask yourselves this question just as we do. It's obviously no more your idea of fun than it is ours.

How much longer is the racket going to go on?

All the prophecies of it ending before November have been exploded. When the invasion came off they told you that Germany was finished. "It won't be long now," they said.

Looks like they were wrong. They're admitting it too. In September they began to hint that the war might possibly last longer than was expected. In October, Sir Walter Citrine said that contrary to the impression of a few weeks ago it seemed probable now that the war with Germany would carry on for a considerable time yet. And Reuter's correspondent, David Friedmann, wired from France,

"Germany is nothing like defeated . . . Most well-informed officers are of the opinion that the war is likely to go on well into 1945."

Prime Minister Churchill himself said in the House of Commons that he reckoned the German war would last until the end of next Spring.

And so it goes on. And you're lead on from autumn to winter, from one year to the next, always being told that victory is just round the corner. Some corner! It's a vicious circle. Never on this wind as we Germans lay down our arms. Get that clear.

Didn't the full stop that the Allied armies came to on Germany's western frontiers give you some idea of how much longer the war was going to last? Your military experts are now talking about advances in feet and inches. Get out your foot-rules and check up yourselves how long it is likely to take you to get as far as Berlin. Something like 18, 19 or 20 years. A cheerful thought.

And yet, back home, they are always talking big about the end of the war and what they are going to do then. With us it's different. We're in the middle of the war, and so for the time being we concentrate on nothing else but war.

MORE TO COME

Maybe you've heard something about our People's Grenadiers, about the Volkssturm—and about the new weapons that we are preparing. You've had a taste of what's coming already. And there's more to come. Lots more. We've got a whole programme worked out for you.

Take a tip. Don't count too much on the war coming to an end very soon. It's still going on, remember. It's not over yet; there's plenty more to come, and meanwhile it won't do you any harm to put in a spot of training. Get tough. You'll need to be.

For you, the war's nothing like over. Apart from this little show going on now, you've still got a job to do in the Far East. And then there are a number of differences of opinion between you and your allies. They'll have to get cleared up somehow some time.

Your blokes who are prisoners of war over here are shooting their mouths off about the war you're going to have with Russia.

Yes, it looks like you're going to have plenty of fighting to do, Tommy.

THE ADVANCE INTO GERMANY is progressing swiftly for these Yanks. They're on their way to safety in prisoner-of-war camps.

"The Main Thing!"

George came home to Hackney, a hero from Holland. He had one leg, one arm and one eye left.

"Is our house okay?" he asked his wife as she met him at the station.

"Yes, George, our house is still all right."

And George went home, and his wife looked after him lovingly. But — it would just happen that way — that very night a flybomb shattered George's house.

When they dug poor George out from under the ruins and the rubble, they found him as chippy and cheerful as ever.

"My poor darling," said his wife, "you've already lost one leg and one arm and one eye, and now our home is gone too!"

"Nuts!" said George, "that's all nothing. They're all minor details. It's the main thing that matters."

"Yes, George." — "And the main thing is that we get Danzig for the Poles!"

The lowdown on the Siegfried Line

The Siegfried Line is not a line at all. Nor is it a wall. It is a thick maze of fortifications, a system of defence works built onto and around the old West Wall of 1939, and stretching far inside Germany, right up to the Rhine and even beyond.

Much of the country it covers is thickly populated and has a dense net-work of railways and roads, very useful in a defence zone. The People's Grenadiers, fighting in this area, have a transport system at their disposal for every need and emergency.

"We've got more than 100,000 workmen on the job of extending and intensifying the defence works," explained an officer of the Fortification Engineers Staff in Cologne. They had been engaged on this work for many weeks, he said, and most of them were local men. "It hasn't been necessary to bring in much labour from a distance," he went on. "Most of the fortifications are close to the towns, villages or farmsteads, and the men on the spot build their own locality's defence-works, tank-ditches and trenches." For special jobs, of course, expert workmen had been brought up from the interior, and they were mainly employed on construction work with reinforced concrete.

Thanks to the R. A. F.

As for the towns themselves, many have been turned into regular fortresses adapted for street-battles. Years of the Allied air terror have rendered considerable parts of them uninhabitable. *And the ruins wrought by the Allies' bombs now go to make excellent barricades and blocks against the Allies' tanks.*

These street strongholds are destined to play an important part in the fighting to come. Burnt and bombed-out houses have been demolished, and razed to the ground so as to open up a wide field of fire for the artillery that has been built into fortresses of reinforced concrete and rubble amid the ruins. Here there are also rocket projectors and flame throwers — among other things — concealed in the ruins as you may later on find out for yourselves.

Some Tips for House-to-house Fighting

Service regulations for house-to-house fighting have been issued by the German Army authorities. They are based on the experiences in Warsaw of Police General von dem Bach and Partisan Specialist Dirlewanger. The tips include:

never move in the streets. Use instead cellar entrances or holes in the partition walls if you want to move from place to place. A fire-bottle is better than an ordinary hand grenade. The heat and smoke it generates has a bigger effect on the enemy than a single explosion.

One important chapter begins with the words, "House-to-house fighting is the sharpshooters battle." Another declares, "in a built-up area there is no such thing as encirclement. There's always a way out."

Try and get hold of a copy of this handbook. There's information in it that may save your life.

Message of hate: copies of Nazi propaganda leaflet called "The Other Side" were found at the scene of the V-1 explosion at Carlton Colville. Inside the leaflet were photographs of alleged Russian atrocities in Germany and articles deliberately aimed at wearing down Allied morale, one of which began; "When is this bloody war going to end?" (Bob Collis/Jeff Gorrod)

1945

During the last few months of the War the people of Lowestoft were spared the trauma of further raids but this did not bring and end to the loss of life. Tragically, three more Allied airmen were killed in two separate crashes within days of each other and only weeks before peace was declared.

4th March 1945: During the night, with a 'Red' alert in place due to the presence of a small number of German Intruder aircraft, a series of explosions was heard between 7.50pm and 9.25pm at the Esplanade. Initially the explosions were thought to be Anti-Personnel Bombs (APBs) as a number of these fragmentation weapons had been dropped by enemy aircraft during their final raids over Britain. In fact the source proved to be much closer to home. Enquiries made by the Police established that the explosions were in fact 12 'thunderflash' fireworks which had been set off as a prank by some sailors who were slightly the worse for drink. The Police report concluded rather drolly *"No evidence of the perpetrators has been forthcoming"*.

14th March 1945: Air operations saw many aircraft crash or force-land in the Lowestoft area during WW2, but on this date at 2.50pm, the town had one last brush with disaster when a lone USAAF B-17G Fortress bomber was seen approaching from the sea, one of its engines suddenly bursting into flames. The aircraft, 44-6570 '2G-P', of the 487th Bomb Group from Laveham, Suffolk was being flown by 2nd Lieutenant Robert H Portsch, a 24 year-old from Bloomfield, New Jersey. He and his crew were part of a massive force of 1,118 USAAF heavy bombers which had set out to attack a host of targets in Germany, including tank and armoured vehicle plants and oil refineries. The target for the 487th BG was a tank factory near Hanover. Whilst en route to the target, 2nd Lt Portsch's No.2 (port inner) engine began to lose power and eventually, unable to maintain their position in the formation, they were forced to abort the mission whilst over Belgium. When smoke began to appear the crew decided to shut down the ailing engine and feather the propeller. Having nursed the B-17 back over the North Sea the crew were just crossing the coast when the engine suddenly exploded in flames.

The now burning bomber, which was carrying a load of eight 500lb HE bombs and two containers of IBs, began a wide circle to the left, back towards the open sea. Parachutes were seen descending as the crew, on Portsch's orders, began to abandon the aircraft, the tail gunner ending up dangling from a lamppost in Victoria Road, Oulton Broad. As the radio operator, 19 year-old Staff Sergeant Douglas Seavert, attempted to escape the B-17 it is believed he opened his parachute too early and he struck the tail unit, tearing a hole in his parachute canopy rendering it useless. He fell to the ground and was found dead near Dell Road School.

The last crewman to jump to safety later recalled how, when last seen, 2nd Lt Portsch had been calmly going through the procedure to set the aircraft's auto-pilot, so that he could release the controls and follow his crew out. By now the B-17 was heading for the coast where it was hoped it would crash harmlessly into the sea. This, however, was not to be. Seconds later the ill-fated aircraft rolled over and dived into a row of anti-tank blocks near Grange Farm, Carlton Colville, where it exploded in a blazing fireball. Wreckage, unexploded bombs and ammunition were strewn all around the farm, and the owner, Mr Herbet Hadenham, had an incredible escape when two 500lb bombs crashed through a building where he was tending his cows, fatally injuring several animals, but without harming him!

2nd Lieutenant Portsch did manage to jump from the aircraft at the last moment, but was now too low for his parachute to save him and his body was found in a tree close to the wreckage of his aircraft.

Courageous to the last: 2nd Lt Robert Portsch's decision to stay at the control of his blazing B-17 Fortress bomber until it was too late doubtless saved the lives of most of his crew and many people on the ground on 14th March 1945 The wreckage of his aircraft was unearthed in 1986, and roads on the Saxon Fields Estate now carry the names of the young USAAF pilot and his radio operator, S/Sgt Seavert. (via Bob Collis)

In 1986 the wreckage of the B-17 was unearthed by workmen laying the foundations for houses on what is now the Saxon Fields Estate, and numerous items were recovered by the Norfolk and Suffolk Aviation Museum at Flixton, near Bungay. As a lasting tribute to the bravery of Robert Portsch, whose selfless actions undoubtedly saved the town of Lowestoft from a tragedy of immeasurable proportions, roads on the new estate were named after the two fallen crewmen and their hometowns in the USA. In 1992 Carlton Colville

Parish Council dedicated a memorial on the estate, containing the details of the 1945 crash.

In 1997 the B-17 Fortress "Sally B" performed a flypast over the memorial after completing its display at the Lowestoft Seafront Air Festival. After the event, in an open letter to the residents of Carlton Colville and Lowestoft, Mrs Dolores Moore, sister of Staff Sergeant Seavert, wrote from her home in Arizona: *"My brother Douglas Seavert was a quiet, sensitive young man, a quick thinker, dependable and thoughtful. It was because of all these qualities he would have appreciated you remembering him and the others as you are doing today. I do. I was an immature 14-year-old when my brother died but I remember reading about the bombing of London and how sad we all felt at the suffering you endured. I know Doug would have felt that way too – he would also have been very angry. Because of that, he would have done all he could to help end the war and being on board that B-17 was the way he chose. Thank you. I want you to know that we 'yanks' are deeply appreciative that you remember that we gave our fathers, sons and brothers in war, too. You've touched my heart with this observance. God bless"*

So close to safety: 19 year-old S/Sgt Doug Seavert died when he struck the tail unit after baling out of the stricken B-17 Fortress bomber over Oulton Broad on 14th March 1945. His sister, Dolores Moore, visited the area in 2008 and was presented with pieces of the aircraft by members of the Lowestoft Aviation Society.
(Dolores Moore)

31st March 1945: At 11.20am the ROC reported seeing a Mustang fighter dive into the sea half mile off Lowestoft. The aircraft was in fact an RAF Mustang from 154 Squadron stationed at Hunsdon, Hertfordshire. The pilot, Flight Sergeant Pritchard, had reported he was having problems with his oxygen system as the squadron returned over the North Sea from a daylight escort operation, and his fighter crashed just short of the Suffolk coast. Rescue craft, including the Lowestoft lifeboat *"Michael Stephens"* and an RAF high speed launch, searched unsuccessfully for the pilot. All that was found at the point of impact was a patch of oil and a flying glove marked with the name "Forsyth".

What makes Flight Sergeant Pritchard's death all the more poignant is the fact that this had been the last operation for 154 Squadron and it was disbanded later that day. Flight Sergeant Pritchard's name is among more than 20,000 RAF personnel commemorated on the Air Forces Memorial to the Missing at Runnymede.

12th April 1945: The last reported wartime 'damage' in Lowestoft occurred at 10.30am, and it came from an unusual source. A short burst of machine-gun fire from a gunner aboard a USAAF B-24 Liberator bomber, one of several in a formation assembling over the town, stripped the branches from several trees in the Notley Road area, but fortunately without hitting property or causing any injuries. It was presumed the American gunner was test-firing his weapon(s) prior to setting out, a duty not normally carried out until aircraft were well out over the North Sea.

30th April 1945: At 1.25pm the air-raid siren ("Wailing Willy" as some had dubbed it) sounded for the last time through the bomb-battered streets of Lowestoft. Five minutes later the 'All Clear' brought the town's long ordeal to a close and on 2nd May it was announced that the air-raid warning system would be discontinued from 12.00 noon. Six days later, on 8th May 1945, Nazi Germany surrendered unconditionally to the Allies and the deadly air war that had raged over Lowestoft, much of Britain and Europe, for six long years finally came to a close.

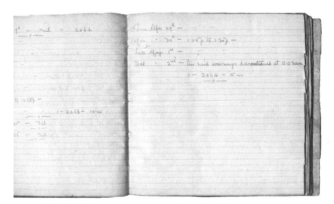

Final warning: Sid Bailey, a wartime Royal Observer Corps Member, could have had no idea his log of air-raid 'Alerts' would last for six years and list some 2,064 warnings. To put the figure into some context, WW2 lasted 2,075 days. One could almost sense the feeling of relief as he made his final entry on Wednesday 2nd May 1945 - "Air raid warnings discontinued at 12.00 hours". (via Bob Collis)

The final statistics make grim reading. Out of 11,830 houses in the borough in 1939 no fewer than 9,433 had been damaged, some on more than one occasion, to one extent or another. In October 1944, by which time the only appreciable enemy action was V-1 Flying Bombs, it was reported that 50 acres of bomb damaged buildings had been cleared by demolition and that repairs to 13,379 properties had been carried out. The same report stated 494 houses were completely destroyed together with 76 shops and premises and seven large public buildings which included the Central School, Wilde's School, the Carnegie Free Library and two Churches.

The German Luftwaffe had during the course of some 105 attacks dropped a staggering 992 HE bombs on the town and surrounding district, together with some 18,000 IBs. Property could be replaced but of course people could not. One hundred and ninety two civilians died in the bombing raids along with 83 service personnel. Seven hundred and thirty one people were injured.

After the ordeal: this is the bleak appearance the Gordon Road area had in 1945, after the rubble from the bomb-sites had been cleared. The white markings on the trees were an aid to vehicles driving with masked headlights in the blackout. Many of the servicemen returning to the town at the end of the war after several years away were shocked at the scale of the devastation. (Ford Jenkins)

The pre-war population of Lowestoft was 44,049 but, with evacuation and mass call-up, that figure fell to 22,000. The massive influx of military personnel, in particular the Royal Naval Patrol Service (RNPS) and the Royal Navy (RN) who were billeted in the town with HMS Europa, pushed the figures back to near the pre-war total.

During the 2,075 days of war the air-raid warning system operated 2,064 times, a total unsurpassed by any other location in Britain in WW2.

On Saturday 5th May 1945 a meeting of senior local police, Air Raid Precautions (ARP) and Civil Defence (CD) officials took place at the Odeon Cinema in Lowestoft. Lord Cranworth, Deputy Lieutenant of Suffolk, paid the following tribute to Lowestoft and the people who had so gallantly defended it:

"East Suffolk was the county in the front line, being one of the nearest to the fortress of the enemy. But it had been a lucky county. They had had grievous casualties and had seen great destruction, but these might well have been greater. But in Lowestoft they had not been lucky; they have had the full brunt of the attacks.

Whether you are the most bombed 'city' or the second or third I do not know, but you have had your share and it speaks wonders for the spirit of the men and women of Lowestoft that the scars in your town are not deeper and that fatal casualties have not been greater. It is perhaps a happy thought that we shall see arise in this town, a 'city' even more worthy than the Lowestoft we have known.

Lowestoft never faltered. Yours was a task of dangers well faced and a job well completed. Your fellow citizens are proud of you all, the whole country is proud of you, and you have good cause to be proud of yourselves."

The air war left the town with a lasting legacy, indeed Lowestoft as it is today has been largely shaped by the results of the damage suffered in WW2. Many pre-war landmarks were lost and, following the demolition and subsequent clearance of many damaged buildings and bomb sites, new roads and buildings were built. In common with many other towns' new estates of council houses were built to address the shortage of housing. Even today, more than 70 years after the first bomb fell on the town, work continues to deal with unexploded ordnance. In February 2010 HMS *Walney*, a Royal Navy Minehunter, operated from the towns inner harbour whilst taking part in a NATO operation to clear the North Sea of unexploded bombs. In the first few days of this operation HMS *Walney* dealt with three 'air dropped' bombs off Lowestoft.

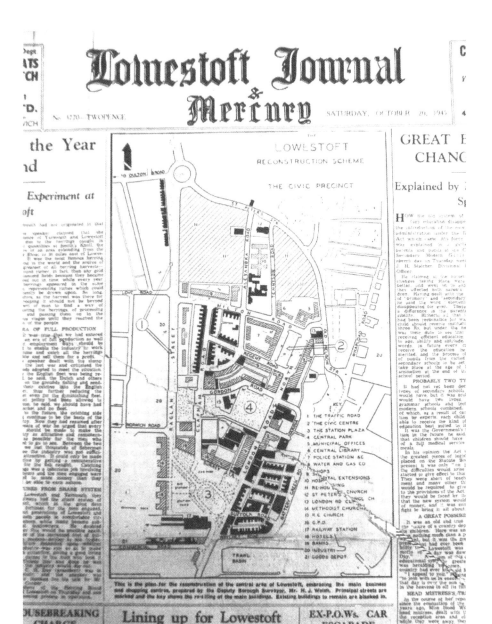

When the war is over: with more than 14 acres of bomb-site clearance on their books, Lowestoft Borough Council wasted no time in outlining its post-war urban renewal scheme. This is the image which appeared in the Lowestoft Journal in October 1945, the shaded areas being those destroyed or damaged beyond repair by enemy bombs. (Archant via Suffolk Library)

Then and now: on 29th September 1940 a 50 kg bomb hit the pavement near Marconi House, on the corner of Grove Road and Battery Green Road. More than 70 years on, the pock-marked frontage and doorway still bear the scars from the hail of bomb splinters which gouged holes in the brickwork. This is but one of the many traces of bomb damage still discernible in Lowestoft. (Simon Baker)

To the people who were affected by, or took part in, the air war over Lowestoft between 1939 and 1945, this book is humbly dedicated.

Roll of Honour
Deaths as a result of enemy air action, listed by date of raid.

The following casualty list has been compiled using the most current information available. Whilst we believe it to be comprehensive any omissions or errors are unintentional.

03/07/40

BASTER	B. E	Civilian
BASTER	E. G	Civilian
BURNHAM	E. S	Civilian
YOUNGMAN	G. W	Civilian

21/08/40

BREACH	G. A	Civilian (died 27/08/40)
BULTITUDE	E	Civilian
FOX	F. C	Civilian
GOSLING	A. W	Civilian
HALE	J. C	Civilian
HARSTON	C. W	Civilian
MURRILLS	G. R	Civilian

29/09/40

BAXTER	I.	Civilian
BLOOMFIELD	F. I	Civilian
ROOPE	J. P	Civilian
THACKER	B. E	Civilian
Fusilier CORFIELD	F.	8th Battalion Lancashire Fusiliers
Fusilier DUXBURY	T.	8th Battalion Lancashire Fusiliers
Fusilier HOLDEN	J.	8th Battalion Lancashire Fusiliers
Fusilier SOARES	F. S	8th Battalion Lancashire Fusiliers
O/Seaman BAIN	A. M	RNPS, HMS Minos
2nd Hd. BLACKIE	T.	RNPS, HMS Minos
Seaman BLAGDON	E. B	RNPS,HMS Minos
Able Seaman SMITH	G. E. M	RN, HMS Europa

18/11/40

FOLKARD	E.	Civilian (died 17/03/44)
HOYLE	H.	Civilian
Pte.MORRIS (Lancaster)	D.	5th Kings Own Royal Regiment

29/11/40

GREENGRASS	E. R	Civilian
NUNN	W. A	Civilian
WRIGHT	G. H	Civilian

04/12/40

2nd LT. LATTER	M. P	514 (Suffolk) Coast Regt.

04/02/41

FORDER	G.	Civilian
SPURGEON	F. M	Civilian
Ld Smn WELTON	M.	HMS Europa

07/02/41

DRAKE	C. W.	Civilian (died 09/02/41)
HAWES	W. J.	Civilian

74

JARVIS	E. A.	Civilian
MANNING	J.	Civilian
MOORE	J.	Civilian
NEWSON	W. E.	Civilian
QUANTRILL	J. R.	Civilian
RACKHAM	H. C.	Civilian
SMITH	G. A. S	Civilian
WILTON	C.	Civilian
WHALEY	F. A. J.	Civilian

15/02/41
| SMITH | R. | Civilian |
| SMITH | W. | Civilian |

16/02/41
| DYKE | L. K. | Civilian |
| POINTER | A. W. | Civilian |

27/02/41
CHEEK	A.	Civilian
CHEEK	B. W.	Civilian
DISNEY	A. E.	Civilian
NICHOLLS	P. G.	Civilian
WEEDS	F. H.	Civilian
WESSON	H.	Civilian

06/03/41
BOLTON	T. J.	Civilian
GREASLEY	P.	Civilian
UPTON	H. F.	Civilian

9-10/04/41
BARNARD	J. M.	Civilian
BARNARD	K. M.	Civilian
BARNARD	P. K	Civilian
CLARKE	B. F.	Civilian
CLARKE	J. F.	Civilian

CLARKE	R.	Civilian
CLARKE	R. E.	Civilian
CLARKE	R. G.	Civilian
CREASEY	E. E.	Civilian
ELWOOD	J. T.	Civilian
MILLER	B. E.	Civilian
MILLER	J.	Civilian
MOULTON	R. W.	Civilian
NORMAN	C. M.	Civilian
OVERY	D.	Civilian
SMITH	A. A.	Civilian
SHERRINGTON	D. W.	Civilian
Corporal GIBB (died 15/04/41)	I.	22 Bomb Disposal Company, RE
Gunner GIBSON	W. W.	129 Field Regt, Royal Artillery
Lieutenant HOARE (died 15/04/41)	G.	22 Bomb Disposal Company, RE
Gunner LAWLOR (died 19/04/41)	M.	129 Field Regt, Royal Artillery
O/Smn HAMMOND	G.	RNPS, HMS Europa
2nd Hd MEADOWS	J. W. R.	RNPS
Seaman SHAW	J. A.	RNPS, HMT Ben Gairn

21/04/41

BROWN	J.	Civilian
TUBBY	L.	Civilian

26/04/41

Wren COATES	F.	WRNS, HMS Minos
2nd Hand HALL	M.	RNPS, HMS Europa

02/05/41

O/Smn CHARLES	T.	RNPS, HMS Europa
2nd Hand JOHNSON	S.	RNPS HMS Europa
O/Smn UNDERWOOD	A.	RNPS, HMS Europa

09/05/41

Asst Cook TUCKER W. H.   RNPS, HMS Europa

12/05/41

DRAKE	R. W.	Civilian
PAGE	V. J. H.	Civilian
PEARSON	J. I.	Civilian
RUNACRES	D.	Civilian
RUNACRES	G. V.	Civilian
RUNACRES	M. R.	Civilian
TRELOAR	F.	Civilian (died 15/05/41)
AC1 WOOLNOUGH	J. V.	RAFVR

26/05/41

BARNARD	L. M.	Civilian
BARNARD	N. J.	Civilian (died 27/05/41)
BARNARD	W. E. C.	Civilian
BRADY	D. M.	Civilian
BRADY	I.	Civilian
CARRON	H.	Civilian
CARRON	L. D.	Civilian
JERMY	F. E.	Civilian
JERMY	M. N.	Civilian
PUTTERFORD	S. M.	Civilian

04/06/41

Asst Cook ROSS W. J.   HMS Europa

13/06/41

Sapper BOWMAN	J.	243 Field Cpy, Royal Engineers
Sapper BROWN	W.	280 Field Cpy, Royal Engineers
L/Corporal DAVIES	G.	280 Field Cpy, Royal Engineers
Sapper FORBES	A.	280 Field Cpy, Royal Engineers
Sapper HALL	C. V.	280 Field Cpy, Royal Engineers
Corporal KERR	R. W.	280 Field Cpy, Royal Engineers
Sapper ROLSTON	L. C.	280 Field Cpy, Royal Engineers
Private DIVITO	R. S.	8th Battalion Royal Scots

L/Corporal GILLIES	H.	8th Battalion Royal Scots
L/Corporal HUNTER		8th Battalion Royal Scots
Private McLUSKEY	H.	8th Battalion Royal Scots
L/Corpral SMITH	R. T.	8th Battalion Royal Scots
Private MUIR	D. A.	8th Battalion Royal Scots
Pte WILBRAHIM	R. W.	8th Battalion Royal Scots
Pte ROBERTSON	J. P.	8th Battalion Royal Scots (died 15/06/41)

22/07/41

CLARKE	B. T.	Civilian
CLARKE	M. E.	Civilian
COOK	P. E.	Civilian
COX	D. I.	Civilian
COX	H.	Civilian
DRAPER	S. E.	Civilian
HARVEY	B. M.	Civilian
REDGRAVE	L. M.	Civilian
REDGRAVE	E. G.	Civilian
RODGERSON	E. G.	Civilian
O/Smn BARTLETT	J.	RNPS, HMS Europa
Seaman BLOCK	A. P.	RNPS, HMS Europa
Ld Smn TAMBLING	E.	RNR, HMS Europa

10/08/41

POWELL	G. H.	Civilian
POWELL	W. H.	Civilian
ROACH	F. L.	Civilian
ROACH	J. M.	Civilian
ROACH	S. A.	Civilian
POWELL	W. G.	RAFVR

13/01/42

ALDRED	D. E.	Civilian
BAKER	W. A.	Civilian
BEARD	E.	Civilian
BEARD	E. H.	Civilian

BEARD	E. L.	Civilian
BONSALL	D. M.	Civilian
BONSALL	E.	Civilian
BULLARD	A. V.	Civilian
CONSTANCE	D. A.	Civilian
COPPING	R. I.	Civilian
CRISPIN	D. R.	Civilian
CROSS	M. E.	Civilian
DAVIES	P. W.	Civilian
EDMONDS	M. B.	Civilian
FLEMING	L.	Civilian
FREDERICK	L. E.	Civilian
GALL	L. A.	Civilian
GARROD	M.	Civilian
GAYFER	G. B.	Civilian
GAYFER	L. B.	Civilian
GEORGE	L. B.	Civilian
GOLDING	O.	Civilian
HAMBLY	S. D.	Civilian
HOOD	I. M.	Civilian
HOWE	D. B.	Civilian
KERRISON	M. G.	Civilian
LACON	N. K.	Civilian
LAMBERT	E. R.	Civilian
MILLS	E. E.	Civilian
MILLS	M. J.	Civilian
MOORE	E. M.	Civilian
MORGAN	A. M.	Civilian
MORLING	E. J.	Civilian
PAUL	D. S.	Civilian
PAUL	E. L.	Civilian
PAYNTER	G. A.	Civilian
PETHERICK	E. T.	Civilian
PINCKNEY	E. S.	Civilian
RAND	M. E.	Civilian
ROBERTSON	J. A	Civilian
SLATER	A. E.	Civilian

SNELLING	D. E.	Civilian
TALBOT	L.	Civilian
THROWER	O. R.	Civilian
WARD	M.	Civilian
WARDILL	W. G.	Civilian (died 29/01/42)
WHITING	B. J.	Civilian
WHITLAM	M. E. J.	Civilian
WINCUP	E. H. D.	Civilian
WOODMAN	D. L.	Civilian
WRIGHT	B. L.	Civilian
WRIGHT	G. M.	Civilian
Pay Lt BAKER	J.	RNVR, HMS Europa
L/Wren BESSANT	L. B.	WRNS, HMS Minos
Skipper BURWOOD	G. R.	RNR, HMS Europa
Ld Wren CREIGHTON	I. W.	WRNS, HMS Europa
O/Smn CUNNINGHAM	S.	RNPS, HMS Europa
L/Smn GRIFFITHS	R. M.	HMS Europa
O/Seaman MUNRO	G.	RNPS, HMS Europa (died 15/01/42)
A/Cook NICHOLSON	J.	RNPS, HMS Europa
Stoker PENFOLD	R. G.	RNPS, HMS Europa
O/Seaman PHILLIPS	F. W.	RNPS, HMS Europa
Stoker SCOTT	G.	RNPS, HMS Europa
O/Seaman TAYLOR	D. F.	RNPS, HMS Europa
Wren THOMPSON	M. I.	WRNS, HMS Minos
O/Seaman URE	J. E.	RNPS, HMS Europa
O/Seaman WALKER	F. E.	RN, HMS Pembroke IV
Stoker WARD	R. A. C.	RNR, HMS Pembroke IV (died 15/01/42)
O/Seaman WATSON	J.	RNPS, HMS Europa
L/Seaman WEST	A.	RNPS, HMS Europa
O/Seaman WILLIAMS	C.	RNPS, HMS Europa

23/01/42

EDWARD	B. M.	Civilian
GODBOLD	J. M.	Civilian
GUTHRIE	J.	Civilian

KING	E. A.	Civilian
RAND	M. E.	Civilian
REMBLANCE	J. K.	Civilian
SOLOMON	M.	Civilian
WALKER	E. M.	Civilian
STERRY	A.	Civilian
STERRY	D. V.	Civilian
STERRY	M. A.	Civilian

01/02/42

BESSEY	H. E. M	Civilian
BESSEY	P. K.	Civilian
BESSEY	P. W.	Civilian

10/02/42

ALLEN	F. R.	Civilian

08/03/42

GODWIN	T. A.	Civilian

01/05/42

WARD	W.	Civilian

05/06/42

HARMAN	A. E.	Civilian
HARMAN	E. W.	Civilian

12/07/42

2nd Hd JENKINSON	J.	RNPS

19/10/42

BIRD	M.	Civilian
BIRD	M. P.	Civilian

06/11/42

BRADY	V. E.	Civilian

12/05/43

BELTON	D. S.	Civilian (died 13/05/43)
BESSEY	E. C.	Civilian
ALBROW	E. C.	Civilian
ANDREWS	E. M. R.	Civilian
BULLEN	W. G.	Civilian
EDWARDS	A. M.	Civilian
FOYSTER	R. L.	Civilian
GIBBS	S. G.	Civilian
GIBBONS	A. E.	Civilian
GOLDACRE	E. E.	Civilian
GOODMAN	G.	Civilian
LING	A. S.	Civilian
LING	F. E.	Civilian
MUMMERY	B. M.	Civilian
MUMMERY	E.	Civilian
NEWSON	F.	Civilian
RANDLESOME	E.	Civilian
SELWYN	E. M.	Civilian
UTTING	B. E.	Civilian
UTTING	W. G. J.	Civilian
WADE	L. O.	Civilian
WATERS	W. H.	Civilian
Seaman BARBOUR	A. R.	RNPS, HMS Europa
Wren CROCKFORD	K.	WRNS, HMS Europa
Act Stwd ELLERY	R.	HMS, Europa
Wren EVERETT	L.	WRNS, HMS Europa
Pay Lt HAYDON	G. A. E.	RNVR, HMS Minos
Act/Stwd HAZEL	J.	RNPS, HMS Europa
Ld Smn HUBBUCK	M.	HMS Europa
Act Stwd LAVERICK	J. G.	RNPS, HMS Europa
W/Man RATHMELL	S. W.	HMS Europa
Petty Officer SMITH	G.	RNPS, HMS Europa
Seaman SMITH	L. L.	RNPS, HMS Europa
2nd Hd STEWART	W. G.	HMS Europa
Ld Smn TUNGATE	L. C.	HMS Europa
Stoker WEBB	J. T.	RNPS, HMS Europa

14/10/44
Lt BASSETT   C. J   Royal Engineers

19/11/44
GRIMBLE   A.   Civilian
RIBBANS   E.   Civilian

DATE OF DEATH UNKNOWN
BROWN   E. A   Civilian